PAINTING
THE
MAP RED

PAINTING THE MAP RED

THE FIGHT TO CREATE
A PERMANENT
REPUBLICAN MAJORITY

HUGH HEWITT

Since 1947
REGNERY
PUBLISHING, INC.
An Eagle Publishing Company • Washington, DC

Cataloging-in-Publication data on file with the Library of Congress
ISBN 0-89526-002-6

Published in the United States by
Regnery Publishing, Inc.
One Massachusetts Avenue, NW
Washington, DC 20001

www.regnery.com

Published in association with Yates & Yates, LLP
Attorneys and Counselors
Orange, California

Distributed to the trade by
National Book Network
Lanham, MD 20706

Manufactured in the United States of America

10 9 8 7 6 5 4 3 2 1

Books are available in quantity for promotional or premium use. Write to Director of Special Sales, Regnery Publishing, Inc., One Massachusetts Avenue NW, Washington, DC 20001, for information on discounts and terms or call (202) 216-0600.

*For Reagan Elizabeth Labert, born November 29, 2005,
and every other son or daughter born and raised while their
father or mother was in the uniform of the United States.
We see and try to thank them for their service and sacrifice,
but do not often have the chance to say the same to you.*

CONTENTS

SIXTY SEATS TO WIN THE WAR

The Strategy for 2006

If you are a conservative Republican, as I am, you have a right to be worried. An overconfident and complacent Republican Party could be facing electoral disaster. Hillary Clinton, Howard Dean, and a host of others could be looming in our future and undoing all the good we've tried to do.

It is break the glass and pull the alarm time for the Republican Party. The elections looming in November 2006 are shaping up to be as disastrous for the GOP as the elections of 1994 were for the Democrats. Most GOP insiders seem unaware of the party's political peril. Some are resigned to a major defeat as the price we have to pay for a decade of consistent gains, which, they think, couldn't have gone on forever.

I have spent the last decade as an optimist about the GOP's prospects, certain that the country's brush with Hillarycare had left a generation-lasting remembrance of what Democrats want to do when they hold all the power. And after 9/11, that belief was joined by a deeply rooted conviction that the Democrats could not be trusted to run the Global War on Terror.

I am still certain that a majority of Americans agree with us—but simply having majority agreement on crucial policy positions doesn't translate into winning elections. Agreement on policy is a necessary but not sufficient condition for winning at the ballot box.

Millions of Americans voted for John Kerry, and they haven't been persuaded by anything that has happened since November 2004 that their choice was wrong. As Mark Steyn put it in a round-table interview I conducted with him, Fred Barnes, and Michael Barone last year, the president has become for the GOP "a problematic figure," largely because the electorate's opinion on him is settled.

As Steyn put it, "People have their view of George W. Bush. Nobody after six years is going to say hey, you know, I listened to a Bush speech last night, and I've got to say, I haven't liked him for six years, but he's persuaded me this time. I think he clearly is, essentially, a 50/50 president, that people who haven't warmed to him aren't going to warm to him now."

Barnes, Barone, and Steyn are, in my judgment, the three ablest analysts of politics on the center-right side of the opinion spectrum. Barone is a prodigious consumer of political data, Barnes is as wired-in as anyone not on the payroll of the White House or the Republican National Committee, and Steyn is the country's finest polemicist.

I began my conversation with them confident that at least one and possibly all three would see opportunities for the GOP in 2006. But in fact, all of them agreed that the Republicans would suffer setbacks, particularly in the Senate. While loss of the House was a remote possibility, they sounded the first clear warning that Republicans could end up shocked and shattered. When that happened to the Democrats on that landslide November night in 1994, I proclaimed, "If it was a fight, they'd stop it." This time we might suffer the beating.

Then congressman Chris Cox, now the chairman of the Securities and Exchange Commission, was one of my guests that night a dozen years ago. He candidly asserted that "anyone who tells you they saw this coming is lying." Democrats had underestimated their weakness, the Republicans their strength. The result was a political earthquake that no one had forecast.

In 2006, it could happen to the Republicans. In fact, that earthquake looks increasingly probable to me. A scandal-plagued 2006 could result in Jack Abramoff–tinged Republicans following the rightly disgraced Congressman Duke Cunningham out of the House and into jail. Conservative Republicans, like you and me, are already disgusted at the inertia of our Senate majority. I fear that disgust, combined with liberal opposition, could help tip the balance for a huge political shift against the GOP. We are losing a once-in-a-lifetime moment.

I don't see a majority of voters changing their minds about the big issues, especially the war. But I do see them changing their minds about the effectiveness of the Republican Party in achieving the majority's goals on key issues.

Voters on the right could sit on their hands by the millions, fed up with the GOP's refusal to govern like a majority, its indulgence of Democratic obstructionism in the Senate, and its general unwillingness to push for urgently needed policies—such as security fencing along the southern border, long-term tax relief, genuine spending control, and the approval of specific judicial nominees. The grandstanding of John McCain and his colleagues in the Gang of 14, the camera addiction of Chuck Hagel, who is always eager to declare the war a disaster, and the antics of loony Lincoln Chafee and other "moderate" senators and congressmen have produced a steady drain on party enthusiasm. Chafee, especially, has stifled the party's hopes to gain seats in the Senate. Donors who gladly poured bucks into the campaigns of John Thune (twice), Norm Coleman, Saxby Chambliss, John Cornyn, Jim DeMint, Johnny Isakson, Mel Martinez, David Vitter, and Richard Burr are passing on the appeals from the National Republican Senatorial Committee's direct mail team, aware that the money is going to the efforts to re-elect Chafee and fellow New Englander and party irritant Olympia Snowe.

And again, the mainstream media will work with the Democratic National Committee to achieve an electoral Waterloo against the GOP.

"The mainstream media is going to be keeping up an assault on Bush, nonstop, as they've been doing for five years," Barone said. "That's their mission in life, to try to destroy his presidency."

"Key question here, Hugh," Barone added, "both for the Catholics, Evangelical Christians, strong religious belief people: who's going to turn out?"

Behind that question is another question: why bother to turn out?

Fred Barnes looked into his crystal ball and concluded, "While Democrats pick up a few House seats, they will not get control of the House, thus no impeachment effort on President Bush. And while they may pick up a Senate seat or two, they will not control the Senate. And while they may pick up a governorship or two, they will not have any sizable lead among governorships. So: small gain that means very little."

I think Fred is underestimating the dangers by a significant margin. There's disarray in the Senate. There are scandals in the House.

There are Democrats boiling with anger and frustration at having been beaten like a drum in three straight elections.

The Soros money machine, on the left, is still out there, pouring massive amounts of money into every race that's even close. And the mainstream media, which couldn't nail Bush with "fake but accurate" documents or "gotcha" last-minute campaign stories about missing ammunition stockpiles, can be much more lethal on a selective, state-by-state basis. An enduring conservative majority could be built within the GOP, in the House, and in the Senate. But it is being frittered away by self-serving opportunists in the Senate and attention-loving back-benchers in the House.

There is still time, though—not just to avoid devastating losses, but to make gains. All it takes is for us to get involved. We need to demand that the party show discipline and leadership. We, you and me, concerned citizens, have to teach the GOP to fight as hard for our goals as the Democrats do for political advantage. The Republican Party needs to listen to us, to get us, the base, back into the game, and to nationalize the election to achieve another conservative revolution as Newt Gingrich did and as Ronald Reagan did before him.

How can this be done? The answer is: with this book, where I intend to outline the goals, strategy, tactics, message, and leadership we need to win. You cannot win elections with only one, two, three, or even four of these big five. You need all five. And we need to demand all five from the GOP.

Step one is articulating the goal. The goal has to be tangible. It has to make sense to activists. It has to be understood as a solution for all that ails them.

The goal has to be sixty votes in the United States Senate committed to ending Democratic obstruction that threatens defeat in war, economic contraction, and a return to an activist liberal judiciary.

The goal has to rally the base and persuade the middle. And there is an obvious strategy to achieve that.

Mark Steyn laid out the winning strategy in typically knock-down straight-ahead style at the conclusion of our round-table:

HH: Mark Steyn, what message would you hit early and often, if you wanted to turn what is at best a 50/50 year for the Republicans around, early in 2006?

MS: Well, I think that their trump card is that these are serious times, and you need a serious party. And whatever you feel about the Republican Party, and there's a lot of disillusionment at the grass roots with the performance of the Republican Congress. Whatever you feel about them, they're still serious on the serious issues, in a way that the Democrats are not. The Democrats have had four years to get serious about the new age in which we live. And they've persistently failed to do so. In fact, they've become more frivolous . . . since the election. I thought a lot of that rubbish in 2004 would be over once the election was over. But they've gotten worse since then. And as long as that persists, they will be un-electable for a certain critical sliver of the American people.

Steyn's grasp of the crucial aspect of the political battlefield in 2006 was followed by Fred Barnes's agreement and his shift to the tactics this strategic difference entails:

FB: I would follow on what has been said so far, and that is: for Republicans, go negative. They have to go negative. They have to scare people about what Democrats would bring. You know, Democrats would run up the white flag in Iraq. Democrats don't want to fight the War on Terror. Democrats want to raise your taxes. That's what you have to do. You have to argue . . . times are pretty good. It turns out we're winning in Iraq, the War on Terror. We haven't been hit again. We're aggressive in waging that war. The Democrats would take all that away. I mean, you really have to go heavily negative.

This is the hard part for Republicans, who are afraid of full-throated, hard-nosed political arguments on national security. They are afraid of complaints that they're "questioning the patriotism of the Democrats." But a liberal party that preaches retreat and defeat deserves political reproach, not "we're all friends here in Congress" politeness.

When Howard Dean declares, as he did in late December 2005, that the war in Iraq can't be won, Republicans need to hang the Democrats with Dean's words. When Dean declares that he hates Republicans, and says that the GOP is a "white Christian" party, Republicans have to call him out as the nutter he's become. When Democratic congressman Jack Murtha called for immediate withdrawal from Iraq, the Republicans in the House did exactly the right thing. They forced a vote on Murtha's proposal and shamed the Democrats into voting against it. The Republicans need to do that again and again. On drilling for oil in Alaska (the great ANWR debate), the GOP needs to talk not just about gas prices but about national security. On issues across the board, the demands of national security should be the trump card to prove that the GOP is the party of seriousness and the Democrats the party of grandstanding and irresponsibility.

A great part of this book deals with the five messages that every Republican candidate needs to internalize and repeat, every conservative talk-show host needs to know and to preach, and every conservative opinion purveyor needs to genuinely embrace without all the asides and reservations about why they are disappointed with this or let down by that. But it's also about what each one of us can do.

All of us have a right to demand effective leadership from our party. For starters, Majority Leader Bill Frist should demand a public pledge from every Republican senator not to side with any Democrat-led filibusters in 2007 and 2008. Any senator refusing to take the pledge should be stripped of his seniority. The same demand should be made of all GOP candidates—and we, the voters, are the ones to hold them to it. It is fine, for example, for Congressman Mark Kennedy, who is running for an open seat in Minnesota, and Senator Mike DeWine, who is running for re-election in Ohio, to vote against ANWR exploration, but not against the up-or-down vote on that issue that the American people want to see. If Republican politicians won't support the policies for which we elect them, then we shouldn't elect them— and we should find candidates who will.

Majority Leader Frist and the president need to make this a national campaign to build a sixty-seat Republican majority in the Senate—a majority committed to action to win the war against terror, defend our free economy, and restore judicial respect for the Constitution. If we do this, we can send the Democrats into political oblivion for a generation or more.

If we achieve a sixty-seat majority, it means we can demand—and expect—that our government will do what needs to be done in the war on terror; that the Senate will approve President Bush's third Supreme Court appointment (if he has that opportunity); that we can pass a constitutional marriage amendment; that we can achieve securer borders, permanent tax relief, and spending restraint. The Democrats' weapon of choice, the filibuster, is an albatross around their necks, and a successful campaign can be waged on ending their abuse of it in time of war.

If John McCain, Chuck Hagel, or any other Republican senator with a glimmer of presidential ambition refuses to take the pledge to end Democratic filibusters, his ambition will be dead. If self-styled civil libertarians like John Sununu of New Hampshire or Lisa Murkowski of Alaska refuse the pledge, they will have endangered their careers (though Sununu's day of reckoning will be much sooner than the just-elected Murkowski's). If Olympia Snowe refuses, she will still win in independent and cranky Maine, but she should lose her position on the Finance Committee. If Arlen Specter refuses, he should forfeit the Judiciary chairmanship he not only loves but in which he has generally been effective.

With a national campaign built on a showdown over national security and ending the Democrats' obstructionism, the Republicans can:

■ Save the Senate seats of Pennsylvania's Rick Santorum, Ohio's Mike DeWine, and Montana's Conrad Burns (if Burns chooses to run)
■ Defend the open seat in Tennessee that Senator Frist is vacating (and in Montana, if Burns retires)
■ Pick up the open seat in Minnesota being sought by Congressman Mark Kennedy
■ Take Democratic seats in New Jersey, West Virginia, Florida, Michigan, Nebraska, New Mexico, North Dakota, and Washington

This "paint the map red" strategy—to nationalize the campaign, as the 1994 campaign was—will work, but only if we demand it of the GOP. The Republican Party needs this bold gambit if it is going to win. Those of us who support the GOP deserve to see it happen. And Majority Leader Frist needs it himself, if he hopes to relaunch his moribund presidential campaign. If Frist does not act, then we should push him out. We cannot afford the Senate to fall into the hands of

Barbara Boxer, Ted Kennedy, Patrick Leahy, John Kerry, Hillary Clinton, Dick Durbin, and Harry Reid.

If, instead of a national campaign, we are reduced to state-by-state slugfests, a dispirited GOP base will ask itself (with good reason) why bother trying again, why give again, why walk a precinct again, why blog again—when they know it will only be more of the same. There are still reasons to do so, of course, but if the GOP deserves our votes it is only because Republican candidates pledge to deliver on their promises on the most important national issues facing this country.

If the GOP fights to end the Democrats' filibusters and to bring action on the pressing military, economic, social, and judicial issues facing our country, we will have taken the first crucial step toward painting the map red, achieving the permanent majority our party needs to prosecute the war, and keeping the nation's defenses in competent hands in 2008 and beyond. In the chapters that follow, I'll show you how we can make that happen.

CHAPTER ONE

THE VALUES WE VALUE

I mean, a part of presidential campaigns, and really part of the large part of [all] campaigns becomes ultimately about values, and not necessarily moral values, although that's important, but what people care about in their life, and whether or not they think a candidate understands them, whether they think somebody's strong or weak, honest or dishonest. It's those types of values....I think Republican candidates that walk in and want to make this a strictly partisan race do so at their peril. I think you've got to make it a values race. And once you make it a values race, then we have a better shot at it...Instead of saying we're going to debate some specific issue, or say this is the Republican plan on this particular issue, I think you have to talk to people at their gut level, where it says what is it...are you like me? Are you a person that cares about the same things I care about? Do you understand what I'm going through?

—**Matthew Dowd**, senior strategist, Bush-Cheney 2004, interviewed January 3, 2006

The goal of the 2006 elections—for conservatives, Republicans, and every American who wants to win the war and continue economic expansion—has to be a United States Senate with at least sixty votes, committed to ending the obstruction of the Democratic left by defeating every filibuster on every issue.

To reach that goal, the Republican Party must nationalize the election, and must make every Senate and congressional contest a part of a national referendum on a single central value supported by the appeals of individual candidates to regional values of regional significance. That single value is the trustworthiness of the president and his party to do what it says it will do, and the unreliability of the Democratic Party on the war and other matters of crucial national importance.

To make this national/regional approach work, the Republican Party must be willing to ruthlessly eliminate from its number those candidates who are either not reliable on the core issues of the party or not trustworthy on matters of ethics.

There are five crucial messages which can be developed at length after every candidate establishes his or her values set, and that values set begins with the president's greatest strength. This is a chapter about the overarching themes that the Republican Party must emphasize if it is to triumph in the fall. Most of those themes reflect regional character types which are as real as they are frequently caricatured.

If there is any doubt whatsoever about the importance of 2006, understand that anything like the decisive loss of the sort discussed in the introduction will make an already formidable and overwhelmingly likely challenge for the presidency by a Hillary Clinton/Barack Obama ticket almost inevitably successful. The results in 2006 will foreshadow the results in 2008 unless some extraordinary event occurs, such as another terrorist attack.

In today's political divide, there is no such thing as an "off year."

The Core Value and the Core Appeal: Trustworthiness on Matters Large and Small

If the campaigns of fall 2006 turn on the value of trustworthiness, the GOP will achieve some gains in the House of Representatives and perhaps stunning gains in the Senate.

This is perhaps the president's greatest strength and the Democrats' greatest weakness: voters trust the president to do what he says he will do and to follow through relentlessly on that promised agenda, even when the odds of success seem remote, and even when the going is rough indeed.

Democrats think the invasion of Iraq and the bloody insurgency present the opening they have long sought to attack the president and through him his party, but that won't be true if the issue is the trustworthiness of the candidates and their party leadership. If 2006 becomes a series of regional contests underneath a banner of a referendum on trustworthiness and an end to obstruction in the Congress, the terrain will dramatically favor the president. The president's commitment to democracy in Iraq, a commitment that has never wavered and which endured three different elections in 2005—the January vote to elect the provisional government, the October vote to ratify the new Iraqi constitution, and the December vote to seat a four-year government—becomes a compelling exhibit in any case to be made for the trustworthiness of the parties as they clash this summer and fall.

Painting the national map red means the ability of candidates and activists to understand the regional nature of politics, and not just the issues set that the GOP majority would like to advance.

The issues matter a great deal, and so do the personalities of the particular candidates. But as senior Bush-Cheney 2004 strategist Matthew Dowd explained in an interview at the beginning of this year, the crucial connection between candidate and voter is on a level of values.

This first chapter is devoted to outlining the values that motivate majorities in various regions across the United States. The Northeast, the Mid-Atlantic states, the Upper Midwest/Plains, the South, the Mountain West, and the West Coast are the broad regions I am concerned with, and within those regions are a crucial set of competitive Senate elections:

The Northeast
Vermont (D) • Maine (R) • Rhode Island (R)

The Mid-Atlantic
Pennsylvania (R) • New Jersey (D) • Maryland (D)

The South
Tennessee (R) • Florida (D)

The Upper Midwest/Plains
Ohio (R) • Michigan (D) • Minnesota (D) • Missouri (R)
Nebraska (D) • North Dakota (D)

The Mountain West
Montana (R) • New Mexico (D) • Nevada (R)

The West Coast
Washington (D)

Twelve of the eighteen "competitive" races for the United States Senate are currently in Democratic hands, which means that the map favors the GOP—decisively, in fact. But that advantage won't matter at all if the candidates are flawed or if the message they carry doesn't connect with the electorate they are trying to reach and motivate.

In the introduction I argued for a national goal of a sixty-seat Senate majority committed to ending obstruction. That's a goal that every party activist, donor, and candidate ought to be able to embrace.

The strategy that gets the GOP to step one of achieving that goal is a national theme on which to build the national framework for the campaign. "An end to obstruction" is the theme, and as the introduction argues, there are some obvious maneuvers available to Majority Leader Frist to advance that theme and focus national attention on it.

That theme must be supported, however, by a values set that every candidate returns to time and time again, and by crucial messages he or she delivers in every setting, to media, to supporters, to opponents, and to the indifferent. Chapters 3 through 7 deal with those crucial messages.

Before those messages are refined and committed to memory, however, every campaign and every volunteer has to be able to convey why the candidate has the same values as a majority of the voters he or she is appealing to. This was the core advice of Matthew Dowd, and he isn't alone in conveying it.

Candidates have to look closely at George W. Bush and realize that they cannot win by running away from the leader of their party. Rather, they have to identify the single greatest strength the president embodies and put it front and center in their campaigns.

That greatest strength is in fact trustworthiness. George W. Bush is a reliable man. He can be taken at his word to do what he says he intends to do or at least try to his maximum ability.

He may not always succeed. Certainly he has not reformed Social Security to provide for that program's fiscal health into the second half of the first century. But he did spend 2005 attempting to persuade Democrats to join him in that effort. And he will no doubt continue to try.

In his first term he pledged a prescription drug benefit. He delivered it. Many in his own party do not applaud this law, citing its expense and complexity. But the point is that the president delivered on his promise.

The same is true for tax cuts, for national missile defense, for tort reform, and for a push for new energy resource exploration. The same is true for judges, at every level of the system. And, since 9/11, nothing has been more certain than the president's unwavering commitment to bring the terrorists to justice or justice to the terrorists.

He warned the Taliban to give up al Qaeda or face overthrow. They balked and he ordered the regime toppled.

President Bush gave an ultimatum to Saddam: Completely and transparently open your regime to inspection and comply with all UN resolutions. Or face overthrow.

Saddam is on trial because George W. Bush can be trusted to follow through on his threats as well as his promises.

This is the crucial "value" with which Republican candidates must identify if they want to spend the next six months on the offensive against their Democratic opponents. It is a strong value, and one that is deeply rooted in our culture: your word is your bond if you are an admirable American.

And on this value of trustworthiness, the Democrats are vulnerable indeed.

Candidate after candidate must begin paragraph after paragraph with the phrase, "You cannot trust Democrats to . . ." The list that could follow is long and persuasive, but it must largely be shaped by the region in which the speech is delivered. If, for example, the candidate wishes to make the point that "you cannot trust the Democrats to let Americans own their rifles and their shotguns," that is a statement much more powerful in Maine and Minnesota—two "blue" states with very high per capita ownership of firearms—than say in Washington state or Maryland. It is no less true in Seattle or Baltimore, but it is much more powerful in Portland or Minneapolis.

Similarly, the statement, "You cannot trust the Democrats to reform extreme endangered species laws" is true no matter where it is uttered, but it resonates particularly strongly in the Mountain West and even in many communities in Washington state devastated by private property rights–destroying listings of the spotted owl, the California gnatcatcher, or the coho salmon.

The obvious truthfulness of statements about President Bush's trustworthiness on a national level provides the context for persuasive appeals to the trustworthiness of various Republican candidates at state and local levels.

How should we set the context for specific arguments about the unreliability of particular Democratic candidates? There are two propositions that again should be part of every candidate and activist's appeal to their base or the undecided.

The first arrived thanks to Congressman John Murtha's December demand for an immediate withdrawal from Iraq.

Democratic Party chairman Howard Dean had plowed the field for Murtha when, on December 5, 2005, he told a San Antonio radio station that the "idea that we're going to win the war in Iraq is an idea which is just plain wrong." Dean continued:

> I've seen this before in my life. This is the same situation we had in Vietnam. Everybody then kept saying, "just another year, just stay the course, we'll have a victory." Well, we didn't have a victory, and this policy cost the lives of an additional 25,000 troops because we were too stubborn to recognize what was happening.

Dean's nuttiness is well known, and his presence at the top of the national party is a continual reminder of the Democrats' general unreliability when it comes to the GWOT, but Dean's explicit defeatism became even more troubling for average Americans because it came after Congressman John Murtha, on November 17, 2005, proposed a resolution to the House of Representatives that declared the "deployment of United States forces in Iraq, by direction of Congress, is hereby terminated and the forces involved are to be redeployed at the earliest practicable date." At a press conference that day, Murtha was very clear about what he was demanding:

> I believe we need to turn Iraq over to the Iraqis. I believe before the Iraqi elections, scheduled for mid-December, the Iraqi people and the emerging government must be put on notice: The United States will immediately redeploy. No schedule which can be changed, nothing that's controlled by the Iraqis, this is an immediate redeployment of our American forces because they have become the target.

To assure there was no doubt as to his position, the first question from a reporter was blunt and Murtha's response was unequivocal:

> **Q:** Congressman, Republicans say that Democrats who are calling for withdrawal are advocating a cut-and-run strategy. What do you say to that criticism?

> **JM:** It's time to bring them home. They've done everything they can do. The military has done everything they can do. This war has been so mishandled from the very start. Not only was the intelligence bad, the way they disbanded the troops. There's all kinds of mistakes have been made. They don't deserve to continue to suffer. They're the targets. They have become the enemy. Eighty percent of the Iraqis want us out of there. The public wants us out of there.[1]

Two weeks later, on December 1, the leader of the Democrats in the House of Representatives, Nancy Pelosi, declared her party to be in support of the Murtha cut-and-run policy:

"I'm endorsing what Mr. Murtha is saying, which is that the status quo is not working and that we need to have a plan that makes us safer, our military stronger, and makes Iraq more stable," she said. "I believe that a majority of our caucus clearly supports Mr. Murtha."[2]

The combined effect of the Dean/Murtha/Pelosi declarations is the simple, undeniable, and powerful truth: you cannot trust the Democrats to pursue victory in the Global War on Terror.

That is the number-one contrast on the trustworthiness issue, and no Democrat should be allowed to campaign between now and then without repeatedly being obliged to agree with this defeatism or denounce it. If the latter, then the GOP candidate needs quickly to discuss how individual differences among Democrats do not matter when the Democratic Party is itself committed to retreat and defeat.

Before moving to regional values within the context of an argument based on trustworthiness, the major premise—Bush is trustworthy on the war and Democrats are not—should be supported by a minor illustration, one identified as such.

Again, there are many obvious candidates for this role, but the best is the most recent and the most obvious, and can be made even more potent by anchoring the recent example in an episode Democrats would surely like to have erased from the nation's memory banks.

First, every candidate must always remind audiences of the importance of the Supreme Court, and of the nature of President Bush's two successful appointments, Chief Justice John Roberts and Justice Sam Alito. (The importance of the courts is expanded on in Chapter Five.)

Before discussing the particulars of the Court, the candidate should ask his or her audience if a man's word should be trustworthy.

In the days following the president's nomination of Samuel Alito, and much to the dismay of Republicans who had history on their side, the Republican chairman of the Judiciary Committee, Pennsylvania senator Arlen Specter, negotiated a hearing schedule with his counterpart on the Democratic side, Vermont's Patrick Leahy.

The president and most Republicans wanted hearings to begin and conclude in December, and there was plenty of time for such a schedule to have been accomplished. (There were seventy-three days between the nomination and confirmation of Justice Breyer in 1994, and only fifty days elapsed between the nomination of Ruth Bader Ginsburg and her confirmation in 1993). Hearings didn't even begin until seventy-one days had elapsed between the nomination of Judge Alito on October 31, 2005, and the start of the proceedings on January 9, 2006.

In exchange for the leisurely pace, Senator Leahy had assured Senator Specter that, absent extraordinary developments, the Democrats would waive their right to delay a Judiciary Committee vote following the conclusion of testimony by one week, meaning that the Committee ought to have sent Judge Alito's nomination to the floor of the Senate for debate on Tuesday, January 18.

But the Democrats broke their promise. They couldn't be trusted even in so small a matter as a week's delay, which they had negotiated away in favor of the very long period from October 31 through January 9 in which to investigate Judge Alito.

Because their collective word became inconvenient, the Democrats simply broke it.

This minor instance of untrustworthiness is a bit of evidence for the major premise, and it also allows for the rhetorical summary that every Republican ought always to remind his audience of: the Democrats cannot even be counted on to count the votes of the men and women in uniform serving overseas.

This is of course a reference to the most shameful moment in modern American political history, more shameful even than Clinton's Oval Office conduct or Nixon's Watergate record: the moment when Gore-Lieberman, abetted by every elected Democrat in the United States, attempted and sometimes successfully so to toss out the lawfully cast votes of the men and women serving overseas who had voted in Florida in the 2000 presidential election.

If you cannot trust the Democrats to count the votes of soldiers, sailors, airmen, and Marines in harm's way, how can you trust them not to cheat in any close election?

Blunting the "Culture of Corruption" Charge

While mounting a campaign based on the positive value of trustworthiness buttressed by the regional values detailed below, Republicans also have to play defense against the "culture of corruption" theme being developed by Democratic leadership as 2006 opened.

The Democrats have been handed a gift by Congressman Duke Cunningham, whose stunning admission of greed, while unique at this writing, provided Democrats an entry point into the rhetoric that accuses Republicans generally of corruption.

To this quite undeniable line of the indictment the Democrats have been busy adding far less persuasive but still potentially damaging paragraphs.

For every trumped up falsehood—the partisan prosecution of Tom DeLay by Democratic prosecutor Ronnie Earle, for example—there are very troubling allegations of genuine crimes such as assertions that various congressmen and or their staffs received illegal pay-outs from the Abramoff machine for off-the-books "favors."

This sort of conduct is distinct from legal campaign contributions and if even one GOP congressman is indicted for bribery via an Abramoff operation, the Democrats' hand in 2006 will be greatly strengthened.

This is why the reform initiative begun in early January by Speaker Dennis Hastert and spearheaded by House Rules Committee chair David Dreier is so vital to defending the GOP against a year of charges.

The changes proposed must be sweeping and their embrace quick and unequivocal. Indeed, if this book appears before the final adoption of such a package of reforms, then the leadership is moving far too slowly to confront the central political threat to its majority.

If, on the other hand, the package is adopted in the first quarter of the year, every Republican candidate ought to take pride in that purposeful move towards transparency. Armed with counterexamples of the bipartisan nature of the congressional corruption problem, Louisiana Democratic congressman William Jefferson has already seen one aide plead guilty to bribery charges in a case that seems almost certain to even the score between Democrats and Republicans when it comes to resignations from Congress for payoffs. Republicans can blunt the worst of the Democratic charges and point to the effective reform of the caucus from within, returning to the trustworthiness theme: "You can trust the GOP to clean its own House. The same cannot be said of the Democrats."

Region by Region: The Tier Two Values Supporting Trustworthiness in the War

Again, if the GOP does well in the Senate races, it will do well in the House. With the exception of the Senate race in Rhode Island, discussed in the next chapter, each of the sixteen key Senate races present great opportunities to build on the national theme via a specific resort to the values identified with the nation's six political micro-climates.

New England Independence

Maine and Vermont are deep blue states, with Kerry tromping Bush by more than 60,000 votes in the former, and by a whopping 20 percent in the home state of left-wing heroes Ben and Jerry.

Yet Republican incumbent Olympia Snowe is a lock to win re-election in Maine, having triumphed in 2000 by a 69 to 31 percent margin. And in Vermont, the retirement of Jim Jeffords puts Socialist Bernie Sanders on the ballot against Richard Tarrant, the co-founder of software company IDX Systems Corp, who is expected to invest more than $5 million of his own funds in the campaign against Sanders.

In the Northeast, two issues cut decisively for Republicans such as Tarrant.

First, most of New England has an attachment to guns, and Sanders's only narrow re-election campaign, 1994, was a result of his pro–gun control votes prior to the election. Gun ownership is a symbol of independence in New England, and of the beloved "flinty Yankee" archetype that even the newcomers to the region exalt in.

Second, the privacy rhetoric usually associated with the abortion rights debate actually carries far further in the region that gave us early patriots. Being left alone by the government is not a value owned by many socialists, so Sanders works overtime to denounce the Patriot Act, and in so doing opens himself to the charge of fecklessness on the national security combined with a socialist's overzealous to meddle in the affairs of the economy both local and national.

Tarrant can bring competitiveness to this race, and with that attention the GOP nationally should be highlighting the embrace the national Democrats have extended an avowed socialist.

Mid-Atlantic Renewal and Reform

Before Jack Abramoff was a household word, there were major corruption scandals throughout America. Three of them came in the Mid-Atlantic region long dominated by Democratic machine politics. In a fourth state in the region, West Virginia, there is no charge against the ancient Robert Byrd, but nearly every town has a Robert Byrd building or stretch of road that stands as a testament to the corruption of the appropriations process in the service of one politician's giant ego.

New Jersey's deeply criminal political culture has disgusted its citizens for years, and the 2004 resignation of Democratic governor Jim McGreevey was only one of scores of public corruption cases to make headlines in the Garden State in modern times.

Across the state line, in Philadelphia, the FBI has been investigating Mayor John Street's administration for years, there is a bipartisan scandal sweeping through the Keystone State legislature, and the entire state legislature alienated voters in 2004 with a secret pay hike that was voted through in the dead of night in July 2005, which led to a powerful voter revolt and the hike's repeal. Disgust with politicians lingers at every level.

In Maryland the conviction of former Baltimore police commissioner and state highway patrol chief on federal public corruption and tax charges in 2004 was just one more milestone in that state's long and deeply corrupt history.

In all three of these states, Republicans have an opportunity to sound the call for reform at all levels of government.

Incumbent Rick Santorum in Pennsylvania and challengers Tom Keane Jr. in New Jersey and Lt. Governor Michael Steele in Maryland will all benefit from squeaky clean reputations married to center-right traditional values of hard work, achievement, and transparency in government contrasted with the machine politics of their Democrat-dominated states. Each of them must continually talk about the machine politics of their opponents even as they contrast their independence of mind and party.

In West Virginia, a blue state that has turned red as the values of the elites in the Democratic Party have headed left, the eventual challenger to Robert Byrd would do well to refuse attacks either on Byrd's racist past or his sometimes doddering appearance.

Rather, the demand for a new start for a new century and a call for investment not in monuments but in a resources industry beset by environmentalists of the radical fringe is what can gain traction.

As Ken Mehlman has pointed out, throughout the Mid-Atlantic there are "resource" voters who know that the states' economic futures depends on access to their abundant natural gifts of coal deposits. These voters honor hard work and honest reward, and resent deeply the national agenda of left-wing activists from the narrow base of environmental activism's extreme.

Marrying the appeal to honesty and transparency to the right of economic self-determination will resonate in the Mid-Atlantic, and the surprise of 2006 could be a GOP sweep of all four of these Senate seats.

One additional note on both the Pennsylvania and Maryland races: First, Rick Santorum's perfect pro-life record matters in the Keystone State, which remains very Catholic, and Catholic in a weekly Mass-attending sense of the word. Democrats recognized this inherent Santorum strength, and have nominated a legacy candidate in the form of state treasurer Bob Casey Jr., a "pro-life" Democrat, to run against Santorum.

Casey's father was a popular governor in Pennsylvania, and a very good man as well, a thorough-going pro-life Democrat. In a June 2000 obituary, *Village Voice* and *New Republic* writer Nat Hentoff summarized the treatment the senior Casey received from the Democratic Party:

Casey's party treated him with disdain. As the 1992 Democratic Convention in New York approached, Casey told me he expected, in light of his policy accomplishments and political loyalty, to be a speaker, maybe even the keynote speaker. But he wasn't the keynote speaker. The honor of nominating Clinton went to New York governor Mario Cuomo, who ignited the crowd by declaring, "Bill Clinton believes, as we all here do, in the first principle of our Democratic commitment: the politics of inclusion."

Casey was not asked to speak. In fact, he and his Pennsylvania delegation were exiled to the farthest reaches of Madison Square Garden because Casey was pro-life. It didn't matter that, under his leadership, state contracts to minority- and women-owned firms had increased more than 1,500 percent in five years, or that he had appointed more female Cabinet members than any Democratic governor in the country, or that he had appointed the first black woman ever to sit on a state Supreme Court. Ron Brown, chief convention organizer and the Democratic Party's symbol of minority inclusion, told Casey, "Your views are out of line with those of most Americans."

Now Pennsylvania Democrats are asking Pennsylvania voters to forget the national party's disdain for Casey Sr., and the national party's abortion rights absolutism. On this point Santorum and the national GOP must be relentless: Casey's alleged "vote for life" would be lost in his caucus. Like Democratic senator Ben Nelson of Nebraska, also a "pro-life" Democrat, Casey Jr. would never be allowed on the Judiciary Committee, which deals with judges and is the committee tasked with abortion issues most directly. Casey Jr. would have almost no influence on any issue of importance to pro-life Catholic voters. Because Casey's party is so extreme on the issue of complete access to even late-term abortion, a vote for Casey is the equivalent of a vote for Hillary Clinton or Barbara Boxer.

And with regards to Michael Steele, the candidate and the national GOP must continually remind Maryland voters of the episode from 2005 where the Democratic National Campaign Committee illegally hacked into Steele's credit records on a vain fishing expedition for anything that could be used against the candidate. Though these Chuck Schumer–supervised staffers could find nothing, the fact remains that this was a felony, a deeply corrupt manifestation of the win-at-all-costs nature of the modern Democratic Party.

The Solid South: God, Guns, and Marriage

In July 2004, Howard Dean—then just a defeated presidential candidate and not yet the chairman of the DNC—told an audience that "sooner or later, voters in places like that [the South] are going to grow tired of voting on guns, God, and gays and start voting on education, health care, and jobs."

Dean was rightfully blasted for his stereotype of southern voters indifferent to economic issues and the quality of their children's education. And Dean's grotesque suggestion that southerners are driven by a maniacal homophobia was also as off-putting to southern voters as it was revealing of Dean's limited grasp of the region and its people.

Yet there was a glimmer of understanding in Dean's tirade: The South is religious, does fiercely value its rights, including those secured by the Second Amendment, and is stalwart in its widespread attachment to marriage and family, and thus resistant to the sort of imposition of hard-left cultural values such as same-sex marriage decreed by courts.

This is why the South is indeed "solid" for the GOP: The real values of the South are best represented in the Republican Party, and those real values have nothing to do with the racism or bigotry that the Howard Deans of the Democratic Party attribute to it.

George W. Bush beat John Kerry by more than 380,000 votes in Florida in the 2004 election, a stark reminder that the 527 vote margin of triumph in 2000 was the result of an artificially suppressed Republican turnout that year, a suppression occasioned by the MSM network's wrongful call of Florida for Al Gore even before the polls closed in the panhandle of Florida that year.

Florida is in fact a "deep red" state, but with a very, very blue liberal representing it in the United States Senate, Bill Nelson. In both 2004 and 2003, Nelson scored an 80 percent approval rating from the hyper-liberal Americans for Democratic Action and a staggering 67 percent approval from the off-the-left-edge ACLU.

Bill Nelson isn't just out of step with Florida. He's out of step with the voters of most liberal states as well.

Nelson is praying that Florida's Thirteenth District congresswoman Katherine Harris is his opponent. Harris won her fame (or notoriety, depending on your partisan affiliation) during the Florida recount of 2000, and her unwavering application of the state law earned her a level of hatred among Democrats exceeded only by that reserved for Bush-Cheney-Rove. Nelson will raise a fortune from her enemies if she is the nominee, and perhaps for that reason, some Florida Republicans continue to scout for a different nominee.

Whether that nominee is Harris or someone else, nowhere is the values component of a race more crucial than in Florida. Put South Beach and Palm Beach and Key West aside; Florida is a deeply conservative state, one with a genuine and enduring affection for the military—the HQ for much of the GWOT, Central Command, is in Tampa, for example—and a strong Bible Belt sensibility. "Florida values, not D.C. poses" should be the GOP's rallying cry. It is a winning, straight-up-the-middle approach, every bit as compelling as a Florida-Florida State game.

The state and national Democrats will try to lead voters into the issues Everglades of Social Security reform, and the GOP must clearly and repeatedly state not just that no senior will ever have his or her benefits cut, but far more importantly, that George Bush can be trusted to protect seniors' income even as he has been protecting their homes and cities and grandchildren from a terrorist attack.

Seniors are the most vulnerable demographic among voters. They need the reassurance and the reminders. With that combination, the red state tide will sweep aside another anomalous blue-coated senator.

There is an open seat in Tennessee that Democrats on their beach days dream about taking away from the GOP with the retirement of Majority Leader Bill Frist.

To advance that cause, Democrats have found their Don Quixote in Ninth District congressman Harold Ford, first elected to Congress from his Memphis district in 1996. Ford is a Penn and University of Michigan Law School grad who brings extraordinary polish to television, and until Barack Obama's election to the Senate in 2004, was certainly the rock star of a new generation of African American politicians.

But Tennessee is not Illinois, and Ford will not be Obama. Where Illinois went for Kerry by more than 10 percent and a half million votes, Tennessee went for Bush by more than 14 percent (a margin of just under 350,000 votes out of fewer than 2.4 million cast.) Tennessee is very much part of the same traditional southern culture as Florida's majority, and will return a new Republican to replace the retiring Frist.

The Heartland: From the Western Reserve to the Western Edge of the Plains

As a native of the city of Warren, in the county of Trumbull in the state of Ohio, the first seat of the Western Reserve, I have grown up aware that the "west" really began at the eastern edge of Ohio, but that Manifest Destiny made the idea of the "Midwest" necessary.

Another term, the "Plains States," had to be added to further differentiate among the various areas of the broad, northern middle of the United States.

"The Plains States are those states located in the Great Plains region, between the Mississippi and the Rockies," writes geography buff John Cletheroe, who also opines that "'The Midwest' is a vague informal term sometimes taken to refer roughly to the region between the Appalachian Mountains and the Rockies, although many people would exclude the westernmost plains states."[3]

The terms might not have much precision when it comes to boundaries or debate-ending consequence when Missouri natives are asked if they are from the Midwest, but for political purposes, the values that dominate from the eastern edge of Ohio through the upper Midwest of Minnesota and North Dakota down through Nebraska and Missouri are all from a common historical legacy of farming and frontier, family and faith. This region was dominated by free-soilers, is the historic heart of the Party of Lincoln, with Abe carrying all of the then existing states of the region except Missouri, and as the years have rolled on, the epicenter of the Civil War that was Missouri has become not only the "geographic center of the nation's population," to quote *The 2006 Almanac of American Politics*, but also a cultural and political cousin of its northern cousins in its majority attachment to the values of the middle states, or the flyover country between the original colonies-states and the Rockies.

In this region, Republicans will fight the half-dozen United States Senate races that will determine whether the party can assemble the sixty anti-filibuster votes it needs to chart a crucial course for the new century.

Republicans must first hold on to the two seats they presently control, with Ohio's Mike DeWine and Missouri's Jim Talent on most Democratic hit lists. Missouri's Talent is comfortably ahead, but

DeWine will face a very strong challenge either from radical Iraq war veteran Paul Hackett or longtime Democratic machine pol Sherrod Brown, a congressman first elected in 1992 from the Akron area whose voting record is as reliably liberal as anyone in the House, with a 95 percent and 100 percent ADA rating in 2003 and 2004 respectively. (DeWine must be hoping that the hot-tempered and rhetorically third rail–oriented Hackett gets the primary challenge as Brown will run a far more disciplined, traditional campaign in a year when Ohio voters may simply be sick of Republicans and the corruption-tainted Governor Bob Taft, who is retiring.)

In Michigan, a state reeling from GM's woes has to consider re-electing the wholly ineffective Debbie Stabenow, widely regarded as an ineffective lightweight who owed her narrow 2000 win to the same GOP turnout–depressing early and erroneous call of Florida for Gore that sent Florida into overtime, and cost John Ashcroft and Slade Gordon their seats that year.

Minnesota's Senate race is an open seat thanks to the decision of the loopy Mark Dayton to retire rather than get tossed out by a disgusted Gopher State electorate. Republican Mark Kennedy is a tenacious and disciplined campaigner and successful businessman who will stay close to popular governor Tim Pawlenty.

Which brings us to Nebraska and North Dakota, two deeply red states with blue senators, Ben Nelson in Nebraska and Kent Conrad in North Dakota.

George Bush carried Nebraska over John Kerry by a vote of 66 percent to 33 percent and North Dakota by a margin of 63 to 35 percent. These are the sort of margins that give even popular figures like incumbent Nebraska senator Ben Nelson pause, and which positively panic a reliably liberal vote like Conrad (a 90 percent ADA approval rating.)

All six of these races could be won by Republicans. All six could also be taken by Democrats. In the absence of a national campaign context, the races will devolve into pitched battles that favor the incumbents, and a showdown in Minnesota over turnout efforts.

But a national campaign anchored in the trustworthiness of the president on the war changes the dynamic completely, and would encourage these traditionally very patriotic heartland constituencies to refocus on the fact that we live in a 9/11 world. Dowd, on the Midwestern battlegrounds:

The interesting thing about the Midwest, which is I think similar to what happened in the South, and then the border states, is that a large part of the population, especially rural and small towns, that were Democrats for years and years, have now decided that their values are more in tune with the Republican Party. It's why Kentucky, which used to be, and for West Virginia, both used to be Democratic states, and then swing states, and now have basically become Republican states. It's because a lot of those rural and small-town folks have finally decided that the party that best represents their values is the Republican Party. The same is true in places like Michigan and Wisconsin and Minnesota, where Democrats always won those races by winning out-state, by winning in small towns, and in the rural areas. Now those areas... [the] upper peninsula in Michigan is a perfect example, where the president, though he lost Michigan, he carried the upper peninsula of Michigan, which is very, very unusual. And the same is true of out-state Minnesota, and out-state of Minneapolis and St. Paul, and in the areas outside of Milwaukee in the rural areas. I think those are advantages, and the trend lines, whether they catch up at this election or not, will tell. But I think the trend lines are good in those areas of growth for the Republican Party.

Dowd is referring to a process of political change that is not tied to particular realignment-forcing issues, but to an accelerating search for common values between candidates and parties and their electorates.

Throughout the upper Midwest there is an open-handed culture of community and straightforwardness that has most of its roots in the life of the farm that dominated the late nineteenth and most of the twentieth century in those states. Even in the urban areas of these states—the Twin Cities, Cleveland, Cincinnati—there was and remains a legacy of church every bit as obvious as St. Paul's Cathedral's imposing presence over the city by the same name. Even Detroit and St. Louis, with their traditional power centers in the black community, have deep religious roots in the African American church, roots that are not remotely comfortable with the social agenda of the left edge of the Democratic Party.

In all of these states, Republican candidates have to aggressively raise the question of whether the voters trust the Democratic candidates to vote like citizens of Ohio or Michigan, Omaha or Bismarck, or whether those pols have gone D.C., like Tom Daschle did.

Kent Conrad has been in D.C. for twenty years, Republicans must stress, and Stabenow's seat mate, Carl Levin, for almost thirty years. What have those men and their party delivered in terms of economic growth or national security, and do their hard-left cultural values really reflect the states from which they sprang?

Crucially, in the red states of the region (and even light blue Minnesota) the decision of the president to campaign in person in the closing weeks of the 2006 election will matter a great deal. It is hard to square a vote for the president and approval of his character with a vote for an obstructionist like Conrad or Stabenow.

And in Nebraska the question must be posed as to why Ben Nelson spends so much time apologizing for the party of which he is a member. If Nelson is embarrassed by the Democratic Party that continually obstructs crucial and necessary policies from the Patriot Act's renewal to the confirmation of judges in step with Nebraska's majority culture, why should Nebraska voters send him back to D.C. for another six-year run that will be spent voting to empower Teddy Kennedy, Barbara Boxer, and John Kerry?

The Mountain West: The Leave Us Alone Voters

In the late 1970s, a name was given to the uncoordinated but numerous protests against federal control of western lands: the Sagebrush Rebellion.

Though its root causes were many and varied, the movement included ranchers and farmers, developers and recreationists who had long been used to the open nature of the land in the west, but who felt imposed upon by the Carter-era influx into the region of environmental activists teamed with low-level federal bureaucrats. A populist revolt sprung up, and the region tilted decisively toward the freedom agenda of Ronald Reagan, himself as authentically western a president as any previous occupant of the White House, despite his birthplace in Illinois and his life in Hollywood. Reagan not only played a cowboy. He became one, and brought into his coalition all the other cowboys and cowboy lovers of the Mountain West (Spare me the *Brokeback Mountain* jokes).

Reagan's triumph ushered in an era during which the members of the Sagebrush Rebellion felt that, even though they didn't come close to winning every battle, at least felt represented in the Congress and of course by the Gipper.

From the time of Reagan's retirement to the election of W, those westerners re-entered an era of eclipse. Because whining isn't exactly a virtue in the Mountain West, that eclipse was largely unremarked upon. Western voters had had their president and their day, and the energy that had accompanied the movement drained away.

But not completely, and the cycle began to run again when, ushered in by Clinton's election and the baffling incoherence of his interior secretary Bruce Babbitt's many clichés—"walk lightly upon the land" for example—even more radical environmental activists appeared, and not just in the not-for-profit world but also within the agencies that were supposed to apply the law, not their own anti-growth, anti-ranching, anti-farming, anti-fishing agendas.

At the same time, the West Coast and the Mountain West began to feel the impact of almost unchecked illegal immigration, and the strain on public services such as schools and emergency rooms as well as the radical rhetoric of some Latino activists combined to form a potent border security movement. Almost overnight the West was again politicized, and again tilting red.

"Here in the Rockies, it's more," Colorado's Governor Bill Owens told me as 2006 opened and we discussed the Mountain West variant of conservatism. "We're more individualistic. There's a concern for stewardship in terms of the great outdoors. We are a low tax region, and Colorado is a low tax state. Taxes matter."

Owens warned about complacency in the face of political change:

I mean, things change, and our party can't always assume that what has been a Republican area in the past is going to be Republican in the future. Colorado, for example, was Democratic. I was the first...I am the first Republican governor in twenty-four years, so we had been a Democratic state with Pat Schroeder, Tim Worth, Gary Hart, Roy Rohmer, Dick Lamm. And then we came along and started to move it towards red, but it's still battleground.

And then Owens moved on to specifically discuss illegal immigration:

There's actually a wave [of illegal immigration] that is washing over the states [in the region]. And so in Colorado, we expect we have about a quarter of a million persons here illegally. In many cases, these are good people. In many cases, these people are here for the best of reasons, but it doesn't change the fact that it's having a huge impact on us financially, in our schools, and our social services. So I think that the issue of immigration is one that needs to be responsibly addressed, and in fact, parts of that border do need a wall, if not all of it.

Low taxes, a respect for individualism, and a concern that the western states are being overwhelmed by a great migration from the south of people who ought to have been stopped at the border, forced to take a number and enter only if legally permissible to do so and then only with the assurance of the sort of employment that allows people to pay their way as the country expands its economy.

All of these issues are tied to a theme of self-reliance, of pay-as-you-go, and of a refusal to ask for or to countenance much in the way of handouts.

The Mountain West wants the rest of the country to work as hard as it does, and that theme—in Senate races in Arizona, Montana, Nevada, and New Mexico—will resonate.

Three of those seats are held by Republicans, and Nevada's John Ensign and Arizona's Jon Kyl are safe bets for re-election as smart, experienced, and very effective voices for the traditions of self-reliance and opportunity.

Conrad Burns in Montana may be more problematic, if he decides to run for re-election. Burns is wrapped up in the Abramoff scandal, and his polling is lousy as 2006 opens, and he may have dropped out prior to the publication of this book. If he does, enter Congressman Denny Rehberg, and the seat remains in Republican hands.

If Burns decides to stick it out, he'll need to cast off all the Abramoff money and ties and do penance for going D.C., but this Marine Corps veteran could probably pull it off with straight talk and help from Bush, who carried Montana by twenty points in 2004. The western voter is tough minded, but also appreciates straight talk. Expect a lot of the latter if Burns re-ups.

The most interesting race is in New Mexico, where longtime Democratic senator Jeff Bingaman wants a fifth term.

The state is narrowly divided, and President Bush's razor-thin win there in 2004—by about 6,000 votes out of three quarters of a million cast—underscores that. Bingaman is not charismatic, and he is a very reliable liberal vote (90 and 95 percent, respectively, on the ADA scorecard in 2003 and 2004).

What makes the race potentially interesting is the illegal immigration issue. If the United States Senate turns back the House of Representative's demand for a border fencing program, expect Bingaman's opponent to try to make this the centerpiece of the campaign. As discussed in a later chapter, the GOP has to be very careful as it raises the issue of border security so as to avoid being branded as racist and anti-Latino, but in a border state, the porous boundary between Mexico and the U.S. is much more easily separated from nativist rhetoric than in non-border states.

Bingaman is a prohibitive favorite, and nowhere is the nationalization of a race more crucial to its success than any long-shot challenger to this incumbent. "Do you trust the Democrats to do anything on the border?" is a question that has to be answered no, and that answer has the potential to destabilize incumbents, though the most likely victim of that fallout would be in a different region, even farther to the west.

The West Coast: Openness, Experimentation, and a Desire Not to Get Blown Up

The story in Washington state, like the story in the Mid-Atlantic races, is a story of a corruption-plagued Democratic Party machine facing an angry electorate, trying hard to turn a lightweight freshman senator, Maria Cantwell, into a serious incumbent.

Cantwell won after the polls closed by a surge in absentees that took her from a loser in votes cast on election day, to a 2,229 vote winner in yet another race deeply tarnished by the election night shenanigans of the networks almost openly rooting for Gore and erroneously putting Florida in the then vice president's column, combined with campaign spending practices that led to an FEC declaration that she had illegally broken the finance rules. She also broke the town bank, spending $10.3 million of her own money in a race in which her campaign spent a total of $11.5 million. Her dotcom fortune went dotbust soon after she eked out her win, and Washington Staters have been wondering ever since about the senator they sent east.

Two years ago Washington state was again the home of an election imbroglio, this one leaving a stench of machine politics that still pervades the state, as Dino Rossi is widely and correctly believed to have been robbed of the statehouse by vote manufacturing as competent as any effort ever mounted by the first Mayor Daley. Rossi could have beaten Cantwell, but declined to run, choosing instead to wait for the chance to claim the statehouse wrongly denied him in the recount of 2004.

But Washington state is allegedly a "progressive" place, and the clean government folks are sickened by the Chicago-style politics that have overtaken the King County elections bureaucracy. Cantwell could well be the sacrifice that the good government liberals offer up.

CHAPTER TWO

HOW BIG IS THIS TENT?

No Longer the Party of Lincoln (Chafee, That Is)

A political party needs to be a tent, and a very big one at that. But it isn't a tent unless there is an "inside" and an "outside," a line beyond which candidates/officeholders cannot go. And candidates/officeholders who are outside that tent not only do not deserve the support of the party, they have to be defeated.

Lincoln Chafee is one such candidate.

The Republican senator from Rhode Island is not a "moderate" Republican, or even a "liberal" Republican. He is a self-described Republican, but to attach the label to him is to drain it of any meaning.

Lincoln Chafee is in fact a "legacy," the term applied to college admittees who had a parent or a grandparent attend the institution. Though it is not always the case that legacies would not have been admitted except for the status of the ancestors, the "legacy" brand carries with it the whiff of non-meritorious selection.

Lincoln Chafee's father, John Chafee, was a liberal Republican, and when he died in 1999, he had served in the United States Senate from the time of his appointment to the vacant seat in 1976 caused by the resignation of John Pastore for the term ending January 3, 1977. John Chafee was reelected in 1982, 1988, and 1994, and served until his death due to heart failure on October 24, 1999. He was the Senate Republican Conference chairman from 1985 until 1999, and was well known for his genuine commitment to conservation.

John Chafee was also a United States Marine, who served from 1942 until 1945, and again from 1951 until 1963. He had also been the governor of the Ocean State. He was, by all accounts, a wonderful man and a fine public servant.

His son may also be a fine fellow, and a tremendous public servant. Lincoln Chafee is not a Republican except in name, however, and if he is the nominee the best thing for Little Rhody Republicans to do in November is to vote for the Democrat. Let me explain why this advice is not inconsistent with my injunction from two years ago that any Republican is better than any Democrat. Lincoln Chafee is the exception that proves the rule.

My 2004 advice was founded on the need for the GOP to control the U.S. Senate majority in order to set the agenda and especially to assure that President Bush's nominees to the federal courts could gain an up-or-down vote. Two years ago there was a real question of whether the GOP would have even the fifty votes it needed to control the chamber with the help of the vice president's vote as president of the Senate charged with breaking ties by the Constitution.

Then came the mandate of 2004, which built on the mandate of 2002, and which returned the Senate to the secure control of the GOP under which it had been until the rip-off of the 2000 election night fiasco, where the early and wrongful call by the television networks of Florida for Gore demoralized and demobilized the GOP base across the country, resulting in the loss to the GOP of at least two U.S. Senate seats—in Missouri and Michigan—and possibly more, in Washington state and elsewhere.

When the smoke cleared from the busted polling machines and the Florida fiasco, the GOP held fifty seats and the Democrats held fifty seats, and then Trent Lott disastrously bargained away his power as the majority party—with Vice President Cheney in the chair—and then Jumpin' Jim Jeffords took his big bounce onto the Democratic side and obstructionism began to define the Democrats.

Lincoln Chafee did not jump with Jeffords, perhaps because any senator with a brain and an ambition beyond his present term can look at the red/blue map and see that the GOP enjoys a large natural majority in the U.S. Senate. George Bush won thirty-one states in 2004; John Kerry nineteen. Do the math and you will understand the natural advantage the GOP enjoys after the Bush Realignment. If elections for the United States Senate gradually follow the state-by-state results of 2004 and state electorates vote for Senate candidates from the same party as the individual they supported for president, then the GOP will slowly raise their majority to sixty-two senators, while the Democrats see their numbers drop to thirty-eight. Of course this will not be a straight-line trend, and some anomalies will occur where a red state sends a blue senator to D.C. and vice versa.

But assuming that anomalous elections occur with roughly equal regularity for both parties, then the GOP should keep its Senate majority for a long time to come, even if the presidency is lost through some unusual circumstances.

So first understand that the GOP doesn't need Lincoln Chafee to keep control of the United States Senate.

The next step in this analysis is to ask how big the tent should be.

My answer is very big indeed: Big enough for John McCain, who is a lousy Republican. Big enough for Chuck Hagel, who wants to be the new McCain. Big enough for Olympia Snowe and Susan Collins of Maine (though Snowe does press against the canvas and in fact leans so far out that you can trace her figure's outline against the wall). And most definitely big enough for Pennsylvania's Arlen Specter, who has actually been a pretty reliable Republican though some still hold enmity toward him for his 1987 vote against Robert Bork.

In short, a majority party needs a lot of the center, and the center needs its own representatives. This is why I adamantly supported Arlen Specter against a conservative challenger in the primary in 2004, and then for chairman of the Judiciary Committee when term limits forced Orrin Hatch to retire from that job.

I don't believe in any litmus tests to be a member of the GOP, and certainly not on abortion. My only litmus test is that a candidate at least be with the party when the party needs him most.

And on this test, Lincoln Chafee fails.

There have been four issues of crucial importance to the party in the past five-plus years that Chafee has served.

The first was the vote authorizing the president to invade Iraq if necessary. Chafee voted against the October 2002 resolution—the only Republican to do so. (Note that Olympia Snowe got this vote right.)

The second vote was the one actually cast on November 2, 2004, in the presidential election. On the day after the president's re-election, *USA Today* ran the following AP story:

Sen. Chafee considers leaving GOP

PROVIDENCE (AP)—Republican Sen. Lincoln Chafee said he would consider switching parties if President Bush is re-elected.

"I'm not ruling it out," Chafee told the *Providence Journal*.

Chafee, known for moderate views that often run counter to the Bush administration, also said he cast a write-in vote for Bush's father, George H.W. Bush, in Tuesday's election. He said it was a "symbolic protest."

The Republican senator said it would have been impossible to vote for President Bush given their opposite views on issues such as abortion, gay marriage, the deficit, tax cuts, the environment and the war in Iraq.

Chafee has opposed the administration's push to drill in the Arctic National Wildlife Refuge and has criticized Bush's handling of the postwar reconstruction of Iraq. He was the only Republican senator to vote against the October 2002 resolution that gave Bush the authority to invade Iraq.

Chafee told the newspaper that he didn't plan to change parties "at this minute."

"I'll have to look and see what happens tonight (Tuesday), the makeup of everything," he said.

After winning races Tuesday in Georgia, North Carolina, South Carolina and Louisiana, Republicans were assured of 53 Senate seats. Undecided races in Florida and Alaska would determine the final sweep of victory for Republicans, who currently have a 51–48 margin, with one Democratic-leaning independent.

Chafee, who was appointed to the Senate in November 1999 to fill the seat when his father, John, died, said if he were to change parties, "it would be with great sadness."

He said he much preferred the elder Bush to his son because the 41st president took steps to make sure the deficit didn't grow and was more of an environmentalist.

Chafee said ever since President Bush has been in office "it's been an agenda of energizing the far-right-wing base, which is divisive."

This was for me strike two and two-and-a-half. Not only did Chafee announce that he hadn't voted for the president, he telegraphed his willingness to defect from the party when the circumstances fit him.

Strike three followed in May 2005, when Chafee joined with John McCain to undercut the Constitution's clear design to afford a president's nominees to the federal bench an up-or-down vote. When Chafee threw in with the "Gang of 14," there was no more question of whether he had any utility at all to the Republican Party. He doesn't.

For the 2004 legislative year, the very liberal Americans for Democratic Action gave Lincoln Chafee a 55 rating, with 100 being a perfect liberal. By contrast, Susan Collins rated a 45, John McCain rated a 35, Chuck Hagel a 20, and Arizona's Jon Kyl a 5.

Only Olympia Snowe was more liberal than Chafee, and she voted for the resolution authorizing war with Iraq and for George W. Bush's re-election. Sure, she joined the Gang of 14—but she got two out of three votes right. Chafee flunked all three.

And, of course, strike four was Chafee's vote against the confirmation of Samuel Alito. Chafee was the only Republican who voted to keep Alito off the Supreme Court.

But there is another far more important reason to exile Chafee as soon as possible.

Senator Snowe is in no danger of becoming the chair of a Senate committee that matters to the national security of the United States. She does sit on the Intelligence Committee, but is outranked by many others.

Senator Chafee is on the Foreign Relations Committee, the third ranking member of that committee behind the venerable Dick Lugar and the maverick Chuck Hagel. Given Chafee's youth, it really is only a matter of time before he becomes the chairman of that crucial committee.

Given his long record of indecision and simple incoherence on matters of foreign policy, that is a risk that is too high to run. There is hardly a position in the United States Senate outside of the Majority Leader and occasionally the chair of Judiciary that commands as much national and international attention as that of chair of the Senate Foreign Relations Committee.

Had Chafee at least supported the president on the invasion of Iraq, as did Senator Snowe, it would be possible to find some argument in support of his re-election, an argument that combined the need for a safe margin in the Senate along with the plea that when the chips were down Lincoln would act like Lincoln.

Yet there is no such argument, and the USA Today article underscores just how self-serving this man is. For a fellow who should be paying the estate tax on every Senate paycheck he receives, that sort of arrogance and purposeful harm to the country's and the party's leader invites the sort of party discipline that, while rare, is sometimes absolutely necessary.

So deep is my dismay with Chafee's antics that I have cut off contributions to the National Republican Senatorial Committee this cycle, as have many others. Blogger Ed Morrissey began the "Not a Dime

More" campaign that had recipients of NRSC pitch letters return them with either a dime or the simple message scrawled across the plea.

The National Republican Senatorial Committee takes care of incumbents first, which means that dollars flowing into those coffers will inevitably be spent on behalf of Lincoln Chafee's re-election campaign. I am unwilling to have my hard-earned dollars go to the cause of re-electing a man who couldn't even bring himself to vote for W's re-election or the crucial vote in the war on terror to date.

There has to be an edge to the tent or the party doesn't stand for anything at all. At a minimum it must stand for national security and for the election of Republican presidents pledged to nominate judges who will curtail judicial appetites for legislative power.

Chafee failed these tests and many other minor ones as well. A vote to send John Bolton to the floor for a vote that never came is not even remotely close enough to obscure the Chafee unreliability index, or to cloud over the looming problem of his seniority in the Senate.

It is time for Chafee to go.

In the aftermath of the revolutions that swept Europe in 1848, the then ruler of Austria, Prime Minister and Prince Felix Schwartzenberg, had put before him the fate of those convicted of conspiring to bring about a revolution, and many pleaded for mercy for the plotters.

"Mercy, by all means mercy," the prince remarked. "Mercy is a very good thing. But first let's have a little hanging."

A big tent is a very good thing, and by all means the GOP must build and maintain such a tent, especially among groups long distanced from the party such as Latinos, Jews, and African Americans. But we have lots and lots of Anglo WASPs and trust-funders already.

To make a party a real party it must also have a little political hanging. And the election campaign of Lincoln Chafee is the perfect occasion to demonstrate that there are limits to the patience of the GOP base.

My campaign against Chafee had begun—on air and in print—
even prior to the confirmation of Justice Samuel Alito. Throughout
that long period of waiting and then the hearings, Democrats used the
possibility of "turning" Chafee and a few other Republicans as a
means of raising money to campaign viciously against the nominee.
Thus does the very presence of Chafee encourage the GOP's enemies
in their most vitriolic campaigns.

Chafee will face Cranston, Rhode Island, mayor Steve Laffey in a
September primary. Laffey has been and will continue to be my guest
on air, and I hope the GOP primary electorate does the state and the
nation a favor by retiring Chafee and giving Laffey a fighting shot at
the general.

But if Chafee slides by, it will be my goal, and it ought to be the goal
of every Republican, to elect a Democrat in Rhode Island.

A closing note: a surface analysis of the voting records of Lincoln
Chafee and Arlen Specter suggest that Chafee is more conservative
than Specter, yet I supported Specter's election over a conservative primary challenger in 2004, the now-president of The Club for Growth,
Pat Toomey.

I did so because of a simple set of calculations: (1) I believed
Toomey could not win the general election, and Arlen Specter could
and did. (2) Rick Santorum would need (and is receiving) the support
of Arlen Specter in his 2006 re-election campaign. And (3) Specter
gets the big ones right.

It is this last point that really matters in a comparison between
Specter and Chafee.

Arlen Specter's American Conservative Union ratings in 2003 and
2004 were 65 and 75, respectively. His National Taxpayers Union ratings for the same years were 65 and 50. Senator Chafee's ACU ratings
were 35 and 40 for '03 and '04. His NTU ratings were 46 and 49.

So Specter is ahead on four of four on the apples to apples comparisons. He gets the big votes right, including in favor of the Iraq War, the president's re-election, and, crucially, for both the confirmation of both Chief Justice Roberts and Justice Alito.

Arlen Specter is a moderate that the GOP must not only learn to live with but to embrace. Majority parties need such breadth, and if he has an iconclast's temperament, so what? He may madden the party faithful on occasion, but he doesn't demoralize it or damage its interests.

The same cannot be said of Chafee.

There are other outside-the-tent Republicans who need to get a shove out the door, chief among them Connecticut's Chris Shays, who is always available to give a negative quote about his party and its leadership. But Shays cannot and never has injured the party. In fact, he's sort of a court jester, and can be amusing in his predictability and his insignificance.

CHAPTER THREE

GOP MESSAGE 1

The Democratic Left and the MSM Have Declared War on the Military. Again.

There is . . . a deep anti-military bias in the media. One that begins from the premise that the military must be lying, and that American projection of power around the world must be wrong.

—ABC News chief White House correspondent **Terry Moran** on the Hugh Hewitt Show, May 18, 2005

The MSM has never worked hard to conceal its opposition to an aggressive waging of the war on terror, including its front in Iraq. With the defeat of John Kerry, that opposition is now fully on display. It will continue unabated throughout the election year of 2006.

The election of 2004 was squarely fought over the conduct of the war, and George Bush won a resounding victory. The elections in Iraq of January 30, 2005, momentarily sealed the idea in the American mind that what we had accomplished in Iraq, despite the huge cost of thousands of Americans killed and wounded, and tens of thousands of Iraqis also killed or wounded, was worth the effort.

But the left had not conceded the point, only the timing. Before four months had passed—four months!—the familiar voices and refrains had begun again, as though the elections in both countries had never occurred.

It first became clear that the MSM was committed to a replay of the end of the Vietnam War—American retreat followed by American defeat—as that set of cues from elite journalism emboldened the leadership of the Democratic Party to make the same agitations toward retreat. The left does not hesitate to deny its past statements when they become inconvenient, and MSM does not hesitate to assist in that whitewashing when necessary.

The assault on the war began with an assault on the American military, and it was an assault with deadly consequences.

The May 9, 2005, issue of *Newsweek* contained the following "Periscope" item:

> Investigators probing interrogation abuses at the U.S. detention center at Guantanamo Bay have confirmed some infractions alleged in internal FBI e-mails that surfaced late last year. Among the previously unreported cases, sources tell NEWSWEEK: interrogators, in an attempt to rattle suspects, flushed a Qur'an down a toilet and led a detainee around with a collar and dog leash. An Army spokesman confirms that 10

Gitmo interrogators have already been disciplined for mistreating prisoners, including one woman who took off her top, rubbed her finger through a detainee's hair and sat on the detainee's lap. (New details of sexual abuse—including an instance in which a female interrogator allegedly wiped her red-stained hand on a detainee's face, telling him it was her menstrual blood—are also in a new book to be published this week by a former Gitmo translator.)

These findings, expected in an upcoming report by the U.S. Southern Command in Miami, could put former Gitmo commander Maj. Gen. Geoffrey Miller in the hot seat. Two months ago a more senior general, Air Force Lt. Gen. Randall Schmidt, was placed in charge of the SouthCom probe, in part, so Miller could be questioned. The FBI e-mails indicate that FBI agents quarreled repeatedly with military commanders, including Miller and his predecessor, retired Gen. Michael Dunleavy, over the military's more aggressive techniques. "Both agreed the bureau has their way of doing business and DOD has their marching orders from the SecDef," one e-mail stated, referring to Secretary of Defense Donald Rumsfeld. Sources familiar with the SouthCom probe say investigators didn't find that Miller authorized abusive treatment. But given the complaints that were being raised, sources say, the report will provoke questions about whether Miller should have known what was happening-and acted to try to prevent it. An Army spokesman declined to comment.

The item was signed by Michael Isikoff and John Barry. The *Times* of London reported the aftermath of the *Newsweek* item five days later, in its May 14 edition:

At least nine people were killed yesterday as a wave of anti-American demonstrations swept the Islamic world from the Gaza Strip to the Java Sea, sparked by a single paragraph in a magazine alleging that US military interrogators had desecrated the Koran.

As Washington scrambled to calm the outrage, Secretary of State Condoleezza Rice promised an inquiry and punishment for any proven offenders. But at Friday prayers in the Muslim world many preachers demanded vengeance, and afterwards thousands took to the streets, burning American flags.

Although the original report in *Newsweek* was small and easily missed, it was re-broadcast by television networks such as al-Jazeera and al-Arabiya and in Pakistan it was quoted by Imran Khan, the cricketer-turned-politician, at a press conference. He said it would strengthen the impression that America's War on Terror was against Muslims.

The most violent protests were in Afghanistan, where the death toll in clashes between demonstrators and security forces reached fourteen after a third day of rioting. Three people were killed and twenty-two injured near Faizabad, in Badakhshan province, when a thousand rioters burnt down aid agencies' offices.

Worshippers in Pakistan poured on to the streets after prayers, chanting "Death to America" and burning American flags. In Jakarta, hundreds gathered noisily at a mosque. Thousands marched through the streets of a Palestinian refugee camp in Gaza.

The unrest began this week after *Newsweek* published an allegation that American military interrogators had desecrated the Islamic holy book in an effort to rattle detainees at Guantanamo Bay in Cuba. The report said that they had placed the Koran on the lavatory inside inmates' cells and had "in at least one case, flushed a holy book down the toilet."

Two days later, cracks began to show in *Newsweek's* account. The *New York Times* reported on May 16 that "*Newsweek* apologized yesterday for printing a small item on May 9 about reported desecration of the Koran by American guards at Guantanamo Bay, Cuba, an item linked to riots in Pakistan and Afghanistan that led to the deaths of at least 17 people. But the magazine, while acknowledging possible errors in the article, stopped short of retracting it."

That hesitation vanished that very day. On May 16, *Newsweek* editor Mark Whitaker issued the following statement: "Based on what we know now, we are retracting our original story that an internal military investigation had uncovered Qur'an abuse at Guantanamo Bay."

Soul-searching among the media lasted less than a day. When White House spokesman Scott McClellan suggested that *Newsweek* could do more to communicate to the world that its story was false, an angry White House press corps jumped down his throat:

Q: Scott, you said that the retraction by *Newsweek* magazine of its story is a good first step. What else does the president want this American magazine to do?

SM: Well, it's what I talked about yesterday. This report, which *Newsweek* has now retracted and said was wrong, has had serious consequences. People did lose their lives. The image of the United States abroad has been damaged; there is lasting damage to our image because of this report. And we would encourage *Newsweek* to do all that they can to help repair the damage that has been done, particularly in the region.

And I think *Newsweek* can do that by talking about the way they got this wrong, and pointing out what the policies and practices of the United States military are when it comes to the handling of the Holy Koran. The military put in place policies and procedures to make sure that the Koran was handled or is handled with the utmost care and respect. And I think it would help to point that out, because some have taken this report— those that are opposed to the United States—some have taken this report and exploited it and used it to incite violence.

Q: With respect, who made you the editor of *Newsweek*? Do you think it's appropriate for you, at that podium, speaking with the authority of the president of the United States, to tell an American magazine what they should print?

SM: I'm not telling them. I'm saying that we would encourage them to help . . .

Q: You're pressuring them.

The follow-up questions were also illuminating:

Q: Let me follow up on that. What—you said that—what specifically are you asking *Newsweek* to do? I mean, to follow up on Terry's question, are you saying they should write a story? Are you going that far? How else can *Newsweek*, you know, satisfy you here?

SM: Well, as I said, we would encourage them to continue working diligently to help repair the damage that has been done because of this . . .

Q: Are you asking them to write a story?

SM: ... because of this report. I think *Newsweek* is going to be in the best position to determine how to achieve that. And there are ways that I pointed out that they can help repair the damage. One way is to point out what the policies and practices of our United States military are. Our United States military personnel go out of their way to make sure that the Holy Koran is treated with care...

Q: Are you asking them to write a story about how great the American military is; is that what you're saying here?

SM: Elisabeth, let me finish my sentence. Our military...

Q: You've already said what you're—I know what—how it ends.[1]

The first series of questions came from ABC News White House correspondent Terry Moran, the second from *New York Times* reporter Elisabeth Bumiller. About the exchange with Bumiller, the *Wall Street Journal's* James Taranto wrote that "the so-called mainstream media have a worldview, formed in the Vietnam and Watergate era, that distorts the overall picture their reporting presents," that the Bumiller hostility showcased that worldview, and that "the cynicism about the military that underlies Bumiller's question is deeply embedded in the mainstream media. That is why the press was obsessed with Abu Ghraib, while it is left to an Australian blogger to track good news from Iraq[2] and Afghanistan[3] in a systematic way."[4]

Of course it was one thing for Taranto to assert that exchanges like those reproduced above evidenced an anti-military bias. It is quite another thing for one of the participants to confirm as much, which is what Terry Moran told me the day after his sparring with McClellan:

> **HH:** Let me ask you something. Major K, a major in the Army who is reporting from Iraq on his blog all the time, says, "all this being said, it is no small wonder that a gulf has opened between journalists and the general public. I think even the most John Q. Sixpacks know when they are being fed a line of blank blank blank. My brother called me a journalist once during a conversation about this blog. I was offended." That is a general impression among the American military about the media, Terry. Where does that come from?

> **TM:** It comes from, I think, a huge gulf of misunderstanding, for which I lay plenty of blame on the media itself. *There is, Hugh, I agree with you, a deep anti-military bias in the media. One that begins from the premise that the military must be lying, and that American projection of power around the world must be wrong.* I think that that is a hangover from Vietnam, and I think it's very dangerous. That's different from the media doing it's job of challenging the exercise of power without fear or favor. (emphasis added)

This is what law professors teaching evidence and trial lawyers summing up for juries call "an admission against interest"—a statement so contrary to the self-interest of the speaker that it has incredible weight and significance. Here is one of the very top reporters in America casually admitting what the center-right has been arguing for the decades since Vietnam: that the elite media in America hate the United States military and the power it projects.

This stunner quickly sprouted legs and ran across the media, drawing nodding yeses and denunciations and everything in between. Less than a week had passed, and another big name D.C. reporter, the *Washington Post's* Dana Milbank, attempted to correct the record about MSM contempt for the military:

HH: Do you think, Dana Milbank, there's a deep-seated anti-military bias in the media?

DM: You know, that comment's gotten an extraordinary amount of publicity. I must say that I've, you know, always found Terry to be perfectly sensible, but I do think he's sort of coming out of left field on that one.

HH: Well actually, he's accusing the media of coming out of left field, but ...

DM: Yeah, right. That's the wrong metaphor. But what I've seen is, you know, look. Karl Rove has put it this way, and Ari Fleischer's put it this way, both of them in the last few months, and have said there seems to be a left-wing bias in the media. I don't dispute that. What they say, though, is the overriding bias is one towards conflict, rather than ideology, and I think they're right about that, too. But the one area where I think people have an overwhelming sense of respect in this business, is the military. Now that doesn't necessarily extend to the civilian leadership at the Pentagon, and for good reason. So, I think maybe it will be more useful to make a distinction between the troops in the field and the political figures in the Pentagon.

HH: Well, after the *Newsweek* story and the riots, and after the Bagram story in the *New York Times* a week ago tomorrow, that's what the context was surrounding it. Did you detect in those

two stories a desire to get the military more fervently than perhaps a desire to get a Republican or a Democrat?

DM: Oh, gosh. I mean, you know, we're talking about the
Newsweek story. You know, it's a Periscope item, and you know,
one of a variety of very small items that they run in there. So,
you know, it's just hard to me to conceive of that that's . . . that
would be Mike Isikoff's purpose in there. And, you know, clearly,
that, you know, the guy who broke the Monica Lewinsky scandal is . . . cannot be credibly accused of having some sort of a,
you know, a political agenda. So, you know, I think we're pretty
equal opportunity in the targets we go after.

Milbank's answer is actually two answers. First there is an attempt
to narrow the anti-military bias professed by Moran and minimize it
by rebranding it as an anti-political-figures-in-the-Pentagon bias, and
then Milbank retreats to the classic "I think we're pretty equal opportunity in the targets we go after," citing the press coverage of Monica
Lewinsky's affair with Bill Clinton.

The MSM is not "equal opportunity" when it comes to supporting
war in defense of American interest. It was Walter Cronkite who
famously affected coverage and thus public opinion of the Vietnam
War. The Museum of Broadcasting puts it this way:

However, returning from Vietnam after the Tet offensive
Cronkite addressed his massive audience with a different per-
spective. "It seems now more certain than ever," he said, "that
the bloody experience of Vietnam is a stalemate." He then urged
the government to open negotiations with the North Viet-
namese. Many observers, including presidential aide Bill
Moyers, speculated that this was a major factor contributing to

President Lyndon B. Johnson's decision to offer to negotiate with the enemy and not to run for president in 1968.[5]

Nearly forty years later, the big names in legacy media are still committed to announcing stalemate and the need for retreat. As the spring of 2005 turned into early summer, Tim Russert, host of NBC's *Meet the Press* and perhaps Cronkite's true heir in terms of reach and influence, on his program on June 26, 2005, used two questions rather than statements to telegraph the media consensus on the Iraq campaign:

TR: Let me show you a graphic, which represents how tough it has been since the war began March 19 of 2003. There have been 1,735 Americans killed; 13,085 wounded and injured; cost is $208 billion; we've been there for 831 days, and still have 135,000 American troops. Does any of that represent, in your mind, misjudgments made by you or the administration about Iraq?

But there are a lot of Americans and members of Congress who believe that fundamental misjudgments were made; that certainly weapons of mass destruction have not been found. The whole notion of how we would be received by the Iraqi people—a few days before the war, I had Vice President Cheney on this program. And this is what I asked him and what his answer was. Let's watch and come back and talk about it.[6]

TR: Do you think the American people are prepared for a long, costly, and bloody battle with significant American casualties?

DICK CHENEY: Well, I don't think it's likely to unfold that way, Tim, because I really do believe we will be greeted as liberators.[7]

TR: Do you think that was a misjudgment?

Cheney parried both loaded questions, and repeatedly returned to the crucial issue of the benefits of removing Saddam and establishing a democratic Iraq in the heart of the Middle East. The point is that by the early summer of 2005 the elite media had committed to a narrative of the Iraq campaign that was designed to send and continually reinforce the messages that the war had been deceptively launched, poorly managed, and was likely to drag endlessly on, and that no amount of progress toward a stable regime, and no inspiring scenes of brave Iraqis showing their purple thumbs, would be allowed to interfere with that narrative. There would be no consideration of the consequences of either having allowed Saddam to remain in power or of pulling out, with the jihadist pipeline now flowing toward Iraq just as it had flowed to Afghanistan in the '90s.

Perhaps emboldened by the despairing-of-quick-victory MSM, but more likely simply because of their deep, deep ideological inclinations, the Democrats could not but join the campaign for retreat, which would mean defeat, even though their thrashing in November 2004 had been followed by the successful Iraqi elections of January 30, 2005.

After a brief four-month period of relative quiet, car bombings in Iraq cued the return of the cut-and-run Democrats, who adopted a dual message: first, that the American military was abusing its prisoners around the globe, and second, that we had done all we could and now was the time to cut and run, that the quagmire created by the mismanagement of the war could not be solved except by sudden and complete withdrawal from the region. House Democratic Minority Leader Nancy Pelosi went so far as to declare the war in Afghanistan over, and her colleague from the Golden State in the Senate, Dianne Feinstein, declared that the war in Iraq was Bush's war.

"It's his war," she shockingly declared as she defended her call for regular updates from President Bush. All but the hard-left fringe of America had believed that every war in which American troops are deployed is our war, but Feinstein's willingness to separate herself from the troops and the victory they were pursuing was just one more bit of evidence among scores of exhibits that supported the proposition that the Democratic Party had defaulted back to its reflexively anti-American military power of the late '60s through early 2001.

The most shocking of all the Democratic rhetorical excesses of last year, and one which should never be forgotten—particularly because it was not rebuked by even a single national Democrat at the time— was Illinois Democratic senator Richard Durbin's remarkable statement on June 14, on the floor of the Senate, and his subsequent contortions.

Durbin read from a report of an FBI investigator that had been released pursuant to FOIA, and used it to attack the American military in the clearest way possible. Claiming that President Bush had ignored the advice of Colin Powell regarding the use of torture, Durbin lashed out at the soldiers in the terrorist detainment camp in Guantanamo Bay, Cuba:

> Imagine if the president had followed Colin Powell's advice and respected our treaty obligations. How would things have been different? We still would have the ability to hold detainees and to interrogate them aggressively. Members of al Qaeda would not be prisoners of war. We would be able to do everything we need to do to keep our country safe. The difference is, we would not have damaged our reputation in the international community in the process.
>
> When you read some of the graphic descriptions of what has occurred here—I almost hesitate to put them in the record, and

yet they have to be added to this debate. Let me read to you what one FBI agent saw. And I quote from his report:

> "On a couple of occasions, I entered interview rooms to find a detainee chained hand and foot in a fetal position to the floor, with no chair, food, or water. Most times they urinated or defecated on themselves, and had been left there for eighteen to twenty-four hours or more. On one occasion, the air conditioning had been turned down so far and the temperature was so cold in the room, that the barefooted detainee was shaking with cold ... On another occasion, the [air conditioner] had been turned off, making the temperature in the unventilated room well over 100 degrees. The detainee was almost unconscious on the floor, with a pile of hair next to him. He had apparently been literally pulling his hair out throughout the night. On another occasion, not only was the temperature unbearably hot, but extremely loud rap music was being played in the room, and had been since the day before, with the detainee chained hand and foot in the fetal position on the tile floor."

If I read this to you and did not tell you that it was an FBI agent describing what Americans had done to prisoners in their control, you would most certainly believe this must have been done by Nazis, Soviets in their gulags, or some mad regime— Pol Pot or others—that had no concern for human beings. Sadly, that is not the case. This was the action of Americans in the treatment of their prisoners.

It is not too late. I hope we will learn from history. I hope we will change course. The president could declare the United

States will apply the Geneva Conventions to the war on terrorism. He could declare, as he should, that the United States will not, under any circumstances, subject any detainee to torture, or cruel, inhuman, or degrading treatment. The administration could give all detainees a meaningful opportunity to challenge their detention before a neutral decision maker.

Such a change of course would dramatically improve our image and it would make us safer. I hope this administration will choose that course. If they do not, Congress must step in.

Public reaction was immediate and vocal: outrage greeted this speech and its obscene comparison of tactics at Gitmo to the methods of history's greatest butchers. But Durbin refused to back down, using spokesman Joe Shoemaker to reject demands for an apology on Wednesday, June 15. Durbin published this statement on his website that day:

No one, including the White House, can deny that the statement I read on the Senate floor was made by an FBI agent describing the torture of a prisoner at Guantanamo Bay. That torture was reprehensible and totally inconsistent with the values we hold dear in America. This administration should apologize to the American people for abandoning the Geneva Conventions and authorizing torture techniques that put our troops at risk and make Americans less secure.

And I remind the White House the Guantanamo Bay scandal has reached such a level of national embarrassment that Senators from both parties are calling for the closure of that facility.[8]

On Thursday, June 16, al-Jazeera ran a story[9] on Durbin that began:

> U.S. senator has refused to apologize for comparing the actions of U.S. soldiers at Guantanamo Bay to those of Nazis, while others have decried or defended the mandate and method used to hold prisoners there.
>
> U.S. Senator Dick Durbin on Wednesday refused to apologize for comments he made on the Senate floor referring to Nazis, Soviet gulags, and a "mad regime" like Pol Pot's Khmer Rouge in Cambodia.

This al-Jazeera story reinforced the obvious and undeniable consequence of Durbin's recklessness: Durbin had given an enormous propaganda gift to jihadists everywhere, not to mention anti-Americans of every stripe.

The uproar in America continued to swell, with more and more active-duty military and their family expressing their contempt for the Democratic whip. Durbin was apparently unaware of the depth of his problem early on Thursday, because he began the day as a participant in the debate on the energy bill, and delivered another clue to his mindset:

> People drive these Hummers. Have you seen them? I personally think if you want to drive a Hummer, you ought to join the Army. But people want to buy them, want to go on the road, and get five or six miles a gallon. And Detroit keeps churning these big, heavy cars. Well, from my point of view, we ought to step back and say as a nation, "Isn't it worth something for us to have more fuel-efficient vehicles so we don't get drawn into foreign conflicts over oil? Is it more important to me to drive a sensible

car, and to spare someone's son or daughter from serving in the military, in the Middle East in a war?

But Durbin wasn't done with his work. He returned to the Senate floor on Thursday night, and tried to explain his Tuesday remarks without apologizing for them, only to be met by Republican senators Warner, Kyl, and Sessions, who sternly rebuked him. Here's the key excerpt from Durbin's second floor statement on Gitmo:

I have heard my colleagues and others in the press suggest that I have said our soldiers could be compared to Nazis. I'd say to the chairman of the Armed Services Committee, I do not even know if the interrogator involved here was an American soldier. I didn't say that at any point. To suggest that I am criticizing American servicemen, I am not. I don't know who is responsible for this. But the FBI agent made this report, and to suggest that I was attributing all the sins and all the horrors and barbarism of Nazi Germany or Soviet Republic or Pol Pot to Americans is totally unfair. I was attributing this form of interrogation to repressive regimes, such as those that I noted. And I honestly believe the senator from Virginia, who I respect very, very much, would have to say that, if indeed this occurred, it does not represent American values. It doesn't represent what our country stands for. It is not the sort of conduct we would ever condone. I would hope that the senator from Virginia would agree with that. That was the point I was making.

Now sadly, we have a situation here, where some in the right-wing media have said that I have been insulting men and women in uniform. Nothing could be further from truth. I respect our men and women in uniform. I have spent many hours, as I am sure the senator from Virginia has, at funerals of the servicemen who have been returned from Iraq and Afghanistan, writing notes to their families and calling them personally. It breaks my heart every day to pick up the newspaper and hear of another death. Now the total this morning, 1,710.

To suggest that this is somehow an insult to the men and women serving in the uniform, nothing could be further from the truth. *But it is no credit to them or our nation for this sort of conduct to occur.* (emphasis added)

In addition to the weasel rhetoric at the beginning, Durbin also made another effort to argue that Colin Powell agreed with him by referencing Powell's public stance against torture—a threadbare effort to sidle up to an American icon and pretend that the icon agrees with you. Still, Durbin refused to confront the central issue: what tactics equaled "torture," and whether the Gitmo interrogations have anything of the Nazis, the Stalinists, and the Khmer Rouge about them.

Arizona Republican Jon Kyl would not allow Durbin to slip away. Kyl blasted Durbin for the "consequences when enemies of the United States seize on even the flimsiest of things to take to the streets and riot."

"Words have consequences," Kyl added. "It is irresponsible and it should not be engaged in, and it should not be countenanced."

On Friday, June 17, as the switchboards in Washington and Illinois offices melted down, Durbin sought the friendly confines of Chicago talk radio, speaking with Spike O'Dell and his co-host on WGN, 720 AM. Here's a partial transcript, omitting mostly the repeat of the FBI text and the argument that Powell was with him (If Powell agrees with Durbin, no evidence was ever produced to support the assertion).

Q: No regrets on the comments you made?

RD: No, I don't, and I'll tell you why. I went to the floor and read a memo from the FBI. This isn't something I made up. It was a memo that was unclassified, was disclosed, and I'm going to take, if I can ask you to bear with me, I'm going to read the highlights of it because it really sets the stage for my comments... [reads investigator memo] It goes on and on and on. I read this into the record because there has been a lot of controversy about what is happening in Guantanamo Bay where we have held 500 to 700 people for sometimes up to two and a half years with no charges. The Supreme Court has ruled that this administration's new interrogation policy under Secretary Rumsfeld violates basic rights and I said if I just read this to you and you didn't know where it came from, where would you think this could happen? In the Nazi regime, in the Soviet regime? Sadly it happened under Americans. Now the point I was trying to make is, we have departed from standards of conduct which presidents of both parties have played by for over fifty years, and we shouldn't be doing this...

Q: So what you just read there was verbatim and when you read it into the record, it was exactly what was there and there was nothing else added to it?

RD: Exactly. And I will tell you what happened afterwards. There was a tremendous reaction, first from the White House, negative reaction, calling my statements reprehensible, demanding some apology to our troops. If you'll listen to this memo, they never say that there was an American soldier involved except an MP guarding a detainee. They talk about interrogators. We don't know if they are from intelligence agencies, private contractors, like Abu Ghraib, we have no idea what they are. But I wasn't disparaging our troops. Our troops are following orders. I'm saying the orders coming down from the top are just plain wrong. . . .

Q: I guess one of the reasons people are having such a hard time with this one, is when comparisons are made and you use names like Nazis and Soviet gulags, when you are talking Nazis there were what, nine million people killed in the camps there. The gulags had about three million and so forth. And I know Gitmo is not the Holiday Inn down there, but I don't think anyone has died down there, have they?

RD: No, that's true. In all fairness, they did not. But I don't believe we were dealing with deaths at Abu Ghraib either. We were dealing with a situation where when people saw the digital camera photographs, they said "My God! Americans should not be involved in that kind of conduct." Now I will not demean or diminish the terrible atrocities that were committed by the Soviets and the Nazis. The points I was, the point I was trying to make there was, if I just read this to you and say "What kind of country, what kind of government would do that," and you'd think of some of the most repressive regimes in history. Sadly this FBI report says its being done by our government. I don't know who in our government. But it should stop . . .

Q: Weren't you trying to ignite a fire, politically speaking, with these comments?

RD: The comments I made were a day before a hearing in the Senate Judiciary Committee on Guantanamo Bay. The hearing was called by Republican senator Arlen Specter. And to his credit, and I said it publicly when I went to the meeting, he had the courage to do it, because we just don't have investigative hearings on Capitol Hill of this administration and this war. We just don't do it. And sadly a lot of things have gone unanswered. My point in taking this to the floor and reading into the record this FBI document, this report from this FBI agent, was to make it clear that the criticisms of Guantanamo Bay go to some very fundamental American values. And that we need to take care not to do things that are going to do damage to our reputation or in any way endanger our troops.

Durbin's continued insistence on "no regrets" only reinforced his critics' anger, and the evidence of that widespread furor broke out all across the web. A retired paratrooper, Blackfive, provided all the contact info for all of Durbin's offices and the comments section of his blog turned up a signed letter from an active-duty soldier which captured the deep ire exploding among the military, their families, and supporters. It is addressed to all United States senators:

> Senators,
>
> I am currently deployed to Kosovo as a member of Task Force Falcon, Multi-National Brigade-East, NATO KFOR. At home I am a teacher in the Kerman Unified School District, providing quality instruction in U.S. History and English/Language Arts to wonderful eighth graders whom I love dearly. I have served in the U.S. Army, Army Reserve, and California Army National Guard for 24 years.
>
> I am currently on orders for 545 days on this contingency operation (Operation Enduring Freedom/Joint Guardian), which means that I will miss everything that my family does for

the next nine months (at least), possibly longer if I am redeployed to another contingency operation, or extended here.

I share the preceding information as a preamble to the subject of this email, so there will be no mistake as to my position, or credibility.

The recent comments of Senator Durbin in reference to the conditions for inmates at the Guantanamo Bay detention facility are as detestable as anything I have ever heard or read concerning members of the United States military. By now these comments have been quoted or aired enough that I need not repeat them here.

The senator's remarks, while apparently intended to apply to only a small number of us, actually hit ALL of us squarely in the heart. To compare any member of the U.S. armed forces with the murderous thugs who ran Hitler's camp system, the Soviet Gulag, or who gleefully slaughtered entire populations in Cambodia, is an affront to all men and women of our military.

Does Senator Durbin really mean to imply that WE are thugs and murderers? Does he really mean to imply that WE treat our prisoners in the same manner, as say, the totenkopfverbande treated prisoners at Sobibor, Belzec, Treblinka, or Auschwitz? Does he really mean that?

If the good senator really does intend to convey this message, then I suggest that he read Eugen Kogon's excellent and heartbreaking study of the Nazi camp system, titled "The Theory and Practice of Hell." I think he should read it, and then decide whether or not his comparisons are entirely accurate. I would also like to suggest that Senator Durbin read Alexander Solzhenitsyn's "The Gulag Archipelago," or "Children of Cambodia's Killing Fields" by Kim DePaul and the late Dith Pran.

We men and women who serve in the armed forces are NOT the jackbooted tyrants that some people seem hell-bent to depict us as. We are many things, but we are not evil. Implications to the opposite effect serve only to undermine and demoralize us as we try with all our hearts to carry out our missions to make the world a better place. If Senator Durbin or any other lawmaker would like to see evidence of, or hear testimony about what we really do, then I suggest a trip to Kosovo. Ask the people here what they think of America and our soldiers. You might be surprised.

In conclusion I would like to remind you that many of the men and women currently running the detention facility at Guantanamo Bay come from the California Army National Guard. They are upstanding and honorable citizens of the state of California, and the United States of America. They are members of the greatest force for peace, or war, that the world has ever seen. I personally know many of them, and they are absolutely not as Senator Durbin portrays them. Senators, I beg of you, stand up for them. Do not allow these reprehensible statements by one of your colleagues to go by the board without censure. He must be called to task on this.

SSG Stephen Pointer S-6/IMO 432nd Civil Affairs Battalion
Camp Bondsteel APO AE 09340

On Friday night, Durbin posted yet another statement on his website:

More than 1,700 American soldiers have been killed in Iraq and our country's standing in the world community has been badly damaged by the prison abuses at Abu Ghraib and Guantanamo. My statement in the Senate was critical of the policies of this administration which add to the risk our soldiers face.

I will continue to speak out when I disagree with this administration.

I have learned from my statement that historical parallels can be misused and misunderstood. I sincerely regret if what I said caused anyone to misunderstand my true feelings: our soldiers around the world and their families at home deserve our respect, admiration and total support.

Even a casual reading of the Durbin record showed a number of things. Durbin was speaking in code, communicating with the hard-left base of his party and their European friends and well-wishers. Here's what he was saying, stripped down to its essentials.

First, Durbin's reference to the Nazis, the Soviet gulag, and Pol Pot's killers was an intentional part of a detailed argument, an argument that equates the killer-prisoners held at Guantanamo Bay with combatants in war, and which asserts that America is acting wrongly and unlawfully vis-a-vis these prisoners. Not only does this undermine the justice of America's cause in the war on terror, it elevates unlawful combatants to the status of legitimate warriors.

Next, Durbin's detailed argument asserts that the conditions and practices at Gitmo amount to "torture," and are part of a pattern that began at Abu Ghraib and continues throughout the world, practices which class the United States among the "most repressive regimes in history." In his original speech, Durbin asserted:

Using their new detention policy, the administration has detained thousands of individuals in secret detention centers all around the world, some of them unknown to members of Congress. While it is the most well known, Guantanamo Bay is only one of them. Most have been captured in Afghanistan and Iraq, but some people who never raised arms against us have been taken prisoner far from the battlefield.

Durbin's argument, coming in this context, implied that the American military had built a global network of Abu Ghraibs/Gitmos, wherein systematic torture of prisoners is taking place, all of it under the control of the United States military. On Tuesday, Durbin had referred to the "torture techniques used at Abu Ghraib and Gitmo and elsewhere" and by Friday, Durbin was making the argument that Abu Ghraib equals Gitmo openly: "This FBI memo points to it. It is the kind of thing that happened at Abu Ghraib."

Of course Durbin had not segregated the criminal conduct by a handful of out-of-control GIs not acting under orders—and already prosecuted and punished—from the authorized conduct at Gitmo and elsewhere. To do so would have protected the military's reputation, but it would have also damaged Durbin's agenda of demonizing the war effort. To advance that agenda, Durbin took a single report from an FBI investigator, inflated its allegations to Abu Ghraib-level criminal conduct, and attributed it to every detention facility used in the war on terror. This was not the simple slander of one interrogator, or one facility.

Durbin's argument also systematically made the case that the threat from Islamists was overstated, and that the reaction to the overstated threat was wildly disproportionate to the real threat. In his first floor statement, Durbin never articulated the threats to Americans from terrorists, but did pause to exclaim in horror that the United States officials "have even argued in court they have the right to indefinitely detain an elderly lady from Switzerland who writes checks to what she thinks is a charity that helps orphans but actually is a front that finances terrorism." Without any explanation of the case or reference to it, Durbin passed on from this portrait of the tyrannical America imprisoning an elderly benefactor of children to the argument that "[a]busive detention and interrogation policies make it much more difficult to win the support of people around the world, particularly those in the Muslim world," thus telegraphing his opinion of American military practices around the world.

Durbin never articulated a defense of any interrogation tactics, never paused over any threat, never recalled the brutality of the jihadists from September 11, to Bali, to Madrid. He never named a single victim of the violence of the jihadists, but instead worried over their conditions, telling his Chicago interviewer, "We have held 500 to 700 people for sometimes up to two and a half years with no charges."

There were originally "no regrets" on Durbin's part because he believes America is deeply committed to criminal conduct in an out-of-control war being waged against individuals who would better be negotiated with. But he beat a tactical retreat from candor on June 21, perhaps because Chicago mayor Richard Daley, whose son had enlisted in the Army, was reported to be outraged at the slander on the military. Durbin's "apology" was more "non-apology" than heartfelt request for forgiveness, a fact masked in part by his tears and in part by the MSM's and John McCain's willingness to declare an end to his public humiliation. Durbin said:

> On June the fourteenth, I took the floor of the Senate to speak about genuine, heartfelt concerns about the treatment of prisoners and detainees at Guantanamo, and other places. I raised legitimate concerns that others have raised, including Secretary of State Colin Powell, about the policies of this administration, and whether they truly do serve our needs to make America safer and more secure. Whether, in fact, some of the policies

might, in fact, endanger our troops, or in some ways, disparage the image of America around the world. During the course of that presentation, I read an e-mail from the Federal Bureau of Investigation, that was discovered to exist last August, and has now been produced as part of a Freedom of Information Act.

After reading the horrible details in that memo, which characterized the treatment of prisoners at Guantanamo, I then, on my own, my own words, make some characterizations about that memo. I made reference to the Nazis, to the Soviets, and other repressive regimes. Mr. President, I've come to understand that was a very poor choice of words. Last Friday, I tried to make this very clear, that I understood that those analogies, to the Nazis and Soviets and others, were poorly chosen. I issued a release, which I thought made my intentions and my innermost feelings as clear as I possibly could. [reads excerpt of the release]

Mr. President, it is very clear that even though I thought I had said something that clarified the situation, to many people, it was still unclear. I'm sorry if anything I said caused any offense or pain to those who have such bitter memories of the Holocaust, the greatest moral tragedy of our time. Nothing, nothing should ever be said to demean or diminish that moral tragedy. I'm also sorry if anything I said in any way cast a negative light on our fine men and women in the military. I went to Iraq just a few months ago with Senator Harry Reid, on a delegation, bipartisan delegation, the president was part of it. When you looked in the eyes of those soldiers, you see your son. You see your daughter. They're the best. I never, ever intended any disrespect for them.

Some may believe that my remarks crossed the line. To them, I extend my heartfelt apologies. There's usually a quote from Abraham Lincoln that you can turn to in moments like this.

Maybe this is the right one. Lincoln said, if the end brings me out right, what is said against me won't amount to anything. If the end brings me out wrong, ten thousand angels swearing I was right wouldn't make any difference. In the end, I don't want anything in my public career to detract from my love for this country, my respect for those who serve it, and this great Senate. I offer my apologies to those who were offended by my words. I promise you that I will continue to speak out on the issues that I think are important to the people of Illinois, and to the nation. Mr. President, I yield the floor.

Most soldiers, sailors, airmen, and Marines commenting on the speech didn't buy Durbin's act of contrition, but he slipped away from sight and the controversy died down—for a few days.

Karl Rove, never one to miss the chance to highlight the collapse of the Democrats on national security, used a speech to New York's Conservative Party on June 22 to illustrate how far around the bend many liberals had gone, and to specifically note the silence of Democratic Party leadership in the aftermath of Durbin's slander on the military.

But perhaps the most important difference between conservatives and liberals can be found in the area of national security. Conservatives saw the savagery of 9/11 and the attacks and prepared for war; liberals saw the savagery of the 9/11 attacks and wanted to prepare indictments and offer therapy and understanding for our attackers. In the wake of 9/11, conservatives believed it was time to unleash the might and power of the United States military against the Taliban; in the wake of 9/11, liberals believed it was time to . . . submit a petition. I am not joking. Submitting a petition is precisely what MoveOn.Org did. It was a petition imploring the powers that be to "use moderation and restraint in responding to the...terrorist attacks against the United States."

I don't know about you, but moderation and restraint is not what I felt as I watched the Twin Towers crumble to the earth; a side of the Pentagon destroyed; and almost 3,000 of our fellow citizens perish in flames and rubble.

Moderation and restraint is not what I felt—and moderation and restraint is not what was called for. It was a moment to summon our national will—and to brandish steel.

MoveOn.Org, Michael Moore, and Howard Dean may not have agreed with this, but the American people did. Conservatives saw what happened to us on 9/11 and said: we will defeat our enemies. Liberals saw what happened to us and said: we must understand our enemies. Conservatives see the United States as a great nation engaged in a noble cause; liberals see the United States and they see...Nazi concentration camps, Soviet gulags, and the killing fields of Cambodia.

Has there been a more revealing moment this year than when Democratic senator Richard Durbin, speaking on the Senate floor, compared what Americans had done to prisoners in our control at Guantanamo Bay with what was done by Hitler, Stalin, and Pol Pot—three of the most brutal and malevolent figures in the twentieth century?

Let me put this in fairly simple terms: al-Jazeera now broadcasts to the region the words of Senator Durbin, certainly putting America's men and women in uniform in greater danger. No more needs to be said about the motives of liberals.

Some small-brained consultant at the Democratic National Committee must have advised the lost and befuddled leadership that Rove's remarks presented an opportunity to turn attention away from

Durbin's slander by arguing that Rove had in fact slandered "liberals," and in quick fashion Senator Harry Reid, the Senate Democrats' leader, and Senator Hillary Rodham Clinton, everybody's favorite in the race for the 2008 Democratic Party nomination, had slammed Rove and demanded an apology.

Before the sun had set on the Democrats' faux outrage, however, New York's Republican governor George Pataki, who had been on the stage with Rove, fired back specifically at Clinton but with a rejoinder that will echo throughout this election year and attach itself to every Democratic candidate:

> I think it is a little hypocritical of Senator Clinton to call on me to repudiate a political figure's comments when she never asked Senator Durbin to repudiate his comments. Senator Clinton might think about her propensity to allow outrageous statements from the other side that are far beyond political dialogue—insulting every Republican, comparing our soldiers to Nazis or Soviet gulag guards—and never protesting when she serves with them.

In other words, where were you, Hillary, when your leadership was slandering the American military and providing propaganda to the al-Jazeera network?

This same question can be posed of every elected Democrat, because with the exception of Mayor Daley, there is no record of any objection to Durbin's slander, just as there was not a single major Democrat who stepped forward in December 2000 to protest the efforts of Gore-Lieberman to disqualify the legitimately cast votes of American military men and women serving overseas during the bitter Florida recount.

The same week that Durbin was apologizing and Rove was scissoring the liberal antiwar gang and Pataki was slamming Hillary, the left's biggest voice made its position on the war known in a Senate Armed Services Committee hearing featuring Secretary Rumsfeld and three top U.S. generals. Said Teddy Kennedy:

> Secretary Rumsfeld, as you know, we are in serious trouble in Iraq, and this war has been consistently and grossly mismanaged, and we are now in a seemingly intractable quagmire. Our troops are dying, and there really is no end in sight. Our troops deserve better, Mr Secretary, I think the American people deserve better. They deserve competency, and they deserve the facts. In baseball it's three strikes and you're out. What is it for the Secretary of Defense?
>
> Well, my time has just expired, but Mr. Secretary, I'm talking about the misjudgments and the mistakes that have been made, the series which I've mentioned. Those are on your watch. Isn't it time for you to resign?"

No end in sight. Quagmire. Resign.

Again, not a single Democrat challenged Senator Kennedy's understanding of the war, and not one rose to defend the necessity of taking the war wherever jihadists gathered, but especially to every region where there might recur a set of conditions similar to those that existed in Afghanistan in the '90s, a refuge where nesting terrorists could plan and execute havoc on American soil, perhaps the next time with WMD.

By the beginning of the summer of 2005, the Democratic Party had been overrun by the MoveOn.Org left, by Howard Dean's people, by Teddy Kennedy's rhetoric. It may be more accurate to write that the

Democratic Party stopped denying its real nature, and instead embraced its inner defeatist, its never-banished "blame America first" impulse.

In the eight months since, the Democrats and the MSM have done little to disguise their heartfelt suspicion of American military power and the American military. They are what they have so often shown themselves to be: a party of bitter hostility to the idea of American exceptionalism and avowed opposition to aggressive pursuit of the Global War on Terror.

These are positions fundamentally at odds with the significant majority of Americans, and as the elections of 2006 approach, expect an attempt to pretend again to be a party committed to national defense. But perhaps not. The left's break-out and capture of leadership within the Democratic Party may lead to a full-throated defense of retreat in the GWOT and other core messages of the left, and if so, disaster waits for the Democrats.

In the aftermath of the MSM/Democrats' spring offensive against the military and the war, Michael Barone wrote of the Democrats that "a party that happily allies itself with the likes of MoveOn.Org and many of whose leading members have lost the ability to distinguish between opposition to an incumbent administration and rooting for our nation's enemies has got serious problems." But Barone made a rare misstep when he concluded: "Especially when it is called on again, as it will be sooner or later, to govern."[10]

The Whigs were never called on again, nor the Federalists, and Canada's Conservatives may well have vanished from the front bench as well, like Gladstone's Liberals. Parties are not always fated to rise again, and the "split" Michael Barone discusses may have become a chasm, with a significant majority of the Dems on the Soros-Moore-MoveOn-Dean-Kennedy-Pelosi-Reid-Durbin side of the canyon. Hillary is going to try to pretend to be on both sides, but that act is already old. There simply aren't enough Americans on the left side of that chasm to elect a president.

The Democratic Party and its liberal/left supporters' negligence with regard to southeast Asia in the '70s brought about the deaths of millions and the enduring Communist governments of Vietnam and Laos and the desperate circumstances of Cambodia. They did not intend that result. In his famous testimony before the Senate Foreign Relations Committee, John Kerry predicted of the aftermath of a unilateral withdrawal of American troops that the United States would have "an obligation to offer sanctuary to the perhaps 2,000, 3,000 people who might face, and obviously they would, we understand that, might face political assassination or something else." His blindness was neither unique nor even notable. They did not see the carnage coming, or the consequence of American retreat from Vietnam as it would manifest itself in Africa, Central America, and ultimately in Afghanistan.

Now the same Democratic Party, the same liberal/left, the same John Kerry and Ted Kennedy and some of the same antiwar protesters grown old, gray, and "respectable," are urging unilateral withdrawal and hauling out their tattered old "quagmire" signs. The same tactics, the same denunciations, the same theater that cloaked the approach of disaster are in play in D.C. once again.

The leadership of the Democratic Party is now committed to a strategy of retreat that will inevitably lead to disastrous defeat and the deaths of Americans here at home. They have reverted to type, and the type is naive and dangerous. Their intentions don't matter, and their predictions can't be trusted. "Sooner or later" could very well be "never," if cooler heads and new leadership doesn't emerge soon.

After a year of steady attacks on the president, the administration, and the war, the MSM has wholly abandoned any claim to objectivity for 2006. They now vigorously campaign for the idea that the invasion of Iraq was founded on an intentional and deceptive manipulation of intelligence, and that the conditions in Iraq—which voted freely in January 2005 for a transitional parliament, for a permanent constitution in October 2005, and for a first-ever governing parliament in December 2005—are too ghastly to admit anything other than that the invasion has been a failure.

The vast majority of MSM elites still don't believe in the GWOT, don't believe in the threat, and don't believe in forward defense. In this regard they are of a piece with the antiwar left that now finds itself running the Democratic Party. Together, they are committed to the repudiation of the Global War on Terror as waged by the Bush administration specifically and to the hobbling of the American military generally.

The stage is set for a six-month brawl between those serious about the GWOT and their opponents in the Democratic Party and the MSM. The American commitment to freedom and self-defense is being tested, and our message is clear: the Democrats and their allies in the MSM have flunked the fundamental test of resolve.

CHAPTER FOUR

GOP MESSAGE 2

The Democratic Left Has Declared War on Religion

Sociologist Peter Berger famously remarked that if India was the most religious country in the world, and Sweden the least religious country in the world, then America is a nation of Indians ruled by Swedes.

Who are those "American Swedes"? Very, very few people admit to being non-religious. Of the 535 members of the House of Representatives and United States Senate, no more than a handful have ever proclaimed they were atheists or agnostics.

The reason for that is basic: Americans believe in God and think their leaders ought to as well. The vast majority of Americans are Christian, and they are incredibly protective of the right of free exercise enshrined in the First Amendment: they do not want to be told how to worship or what to believe, and they cannot imagine telling a fellow American how to worship or what to believe. It is a remarkable and strong consensus position in the country.

In recent decades, though, the left has set out to de-legitimize a large slice of religious belief in America—the beliefs of those Americans, regardless of denomination, who hold that God is interested in the unborn and wants the unborn to be born, not aborted.

In the aftermath of the staggeringly unwise and terribly reasoned 1973 Supreme Court decision in *Roe v. Wade*, this slice of the religious in America began to organize in order to influence politics. In particular, this slice of the religious wanted *Roe v. Wade* overturned, and control of the abortion issue returned to the state legislatures, where it had resided until the Supreme Court made its infamous decision.

The desire to overturn *Roe v. Wade* fueled the decisions of some Christian pastors—specifically televangelists Jerry Falwell and Pat Robertson—to organize political movements. In their cases, the Moral Majority and the Christian Coalition quickly came to represent the political agendas of primarily white evangelicals, and helped propel Ronald Reagan to the White House.

The early successes of these two groups also brought huge attention to Falwell and Robertson, and they were not particularly deft at negotiating the complexity of public communication beyond their own base. Often they sounded notes that struck majorities of American as outside of the great consensus articulated above. Most infamously, the pair appeared together on Robertson's television show in the aftermath of 9/11 and seemed to argue that God had removed His protection from the United States as punishment for America's declining morals. This jarring bit of odd theology and out-of-the-mainstream understanding of a malevolent plot that killed 3,000

Americans seemed to cement then and there the idea that there is a wacky "religious right" in the United States, to be feared and attacked at every turn.

What Falwell and Robertson gave to the left were a couple of easy and big targets they have never been willing to take down, because neither is the retiring type. Many on the left, discouraged especially by the elections of 2000, 2002, and 2004, have decided that the path back to power depends in large part on persuading a majority of American voters that the "religious right" is organized behind the banner of Falwell and Robertson, and that its agenda is as radical and expansive as could be imagined.

The effort to demonize an ill-defined "religious right" began with attacks on President Bush's nominees to the federal bench, an offensive against center-right jurists and would-be jurists. This morphed into a free-floating refrain of almost rote appearance and sustained vehemence: the attack on the "Christian right," or as the more extreme leftists refer to it, "the American Taliban."

Hardly a week goes by without some major Democratic politician or lefty pundit denouncing again and again in the harshest terms the rise of this feared group. In the first few months of last year, *New York Times* writers Maureen Dowd, Frank Rich, Nicholas Kristoff, and Paul Krugman all routinely editorialized about the menace of this group. Leading center-left intellectuals picked up the refrain as well, including Christopher Hitchens and Peter Beinart. The off-the-edge lefties at Air America painted in the starkest terms the evil that was growing in the land, and Harry Reid and Nancy Pelosi led their Democratic elected colleagues in attack after attack on so-called "extremists" of the religious right.

The decision to re-energize a party base dispirited after the pummeling of 2004 seems almost to have been accidental. In the immediate aftermath of the crushing Bush win in November 2004, a shattered Democratic elite spoke mournfully about its estrangement from the "values voters" who had declared so decisively for W.

"Values voters" was shorthand for regular church attenders, but in late May 2006, my colleague on the radio, Dennis Prager, finally figured out how to define not only the "values voter," but also the "religious right" as understood by the Democrats, their candidates, and their consultants.

The American people are not divided between those who believe in God and those who don't, Dennis argued. Almost all Americans believe in God, he pointed out.

But Americans are deeply divided over the issue of whether the Bible is of divine or human origin. Those who believe the Bible's text is divine in origin, and is thus not subject to revision, are very, very different from those who believe the Bible was cobbled together by fallible men, importing their own assumptions and pre-modern superstitions into their accounts of God's design. The latter group believes in God, but they don't believe the Bible authoritatively conveys God's plans and commands.

Dennis first laid out this distinction in a debate with Harvard Law professor Alan Dershowitz in front of a largely liberal audience on the west side of New York. Though they had been locked in heated and constant argument for a long time, Dershowitz stopped the moment Dennis put forward this proposition, and told the crowd that for the first time that night, he and Dennis were in agreement.

Dennis's distinction does help us define "the values voter" very well, and also the Democrats' difficulty in reclaiming a foothold among them. It is very, very difficult to appeal to these "values voters" when Democratic elites, for example, are at best rhetorically supportive of defending marriage as limited by law and nature to one man and one woman. Millions of "values voters" are 100 percent supportive of the civil liberties of gay and lesbian people, and can aggressively

defend the rights of gays and lesbians to respect and dignity and support their complete and essential status as citizens, even as the "values
voter" believes in the wrongness of intimacy outside of traditional
marriage.

The Democratic activist who proclaims that same-sex marriage is
an essential civil liberty and a core principle of the Democratic Party
thus erects a nearly impassible barrier between his party and these
"values voters."

The same barrier keeps out "values voters" who believe that the
Ten Commandments deserve an honored place in public life, that
Christmas crèche scenes and crosses embedded in city seals or long
erected on high places send appropriate messages that cannot reasonably be understood to convey official "endorsement" of
Christianity as an "established" religion. The "values voters" think
church expansions should be encouraged, not obstructed by grasping
city planners, that prayer before high school commencement is a fine
thing, and that clubs of a religious origin and mission ought to be welcomed on the same basis and with the same rights as secular
extra-curricular activities.

The "values voters" like the Boy Scouts and Catholic hospitals and
unusually garbed ultra-orthodox Jews and Mormon missionaries on
bikes. They are comfortable with deep religious belief, and supremely
tolerant of all sects and varieties of faith, even as they claim that their
understanding of those divine texts is the correct understanding.

The "values voters" hate to be cast as haters, especially by haters,
and feel a welling frustration with the left's attempt to define their tens
of millions as mere thousands. They reject, increasingly via political
action, the attempt by a small percentage of hard-left activists and
polemicists, backed by lawyers and relatively recent legal doctrines,
to drive them from the public square and define them as the danger
to America's future.

The evolution of the left's contempt for people of faith, from Marx-ordained hatred of religious belief in general and Christianity in particular to the dominant though usually unspoken attitude of the Democratic Party's elite, is a study in the ability of a few to push the many in the direction of intolerance. The old Democratic Party—the one of just forty years ago—was built on the backs of the faithful Catholic population, the weekly Mass-attending, children in parochial school, and dads in the Knights of Columbus Catholics of the Northeast and Midwest, of a dozen different ethnicities but only one true Church. How it came to pass that a majority of Catholic voters sided with George W. Bush in November 2004, when his opponent was a Catholic, is a long, strange story of small steps left, then left again, then left, left, left again.

Make no mistake. The Roman Catholic Church's central doctrines have not moved in the last forty years, even as the changes brought about by Vatican II did change much of the surface of worship.

But the Democratic Party, once fully familiar with and largely devoted to those doctrines, has hurried away from them. In so doing, it left traditional Catholic voters no choice but to survey their options and vote their consciences.

The inescapable momentum of the abortion decisions to the abortion-on-demand world we live in today and, much more recently, the assault on traditional marriage and the rush to end the lives of the elderly infirm and the deeply disabled, has shocked a majority of Catholics. They now are at the point where they can no longer avoid seeing in the Democratic Party the antithesis of their collective catechism.

This is the most important development of the new political dynamics in the country. The Democratic Party is publicly pledged to position after position that the Roman Catholic Church condemns as grievous sin, and not only does the Democratic Party no longer try to change the subject, its leading voices now wish to change instead the Roman Catholic Church.

More than a six years before he succeeded John Paul II as pope, Benedict XVI, then Cardinal Joseph Ratzinger, sat for many days in an extended interview with noted German journalist and skeptic Peter Seewald, and the conversation appeared as a book, *Salt of the Earth: The Church at the End of the Millennium*.

Reviewing the book for *Christianity Today*, Father Richard John Neuhaus, founder and editor of *First Things*, noted that Benedict XVI was "not above addressing the issues that preoccupy the popular press," and quotes the then cardinal as referring to "the canon of criticism— women's ordination, contraception, celibacy, and the remarriage to divorced persons."

That short phrase, "the canon of criticism," conveyed accurately that the Roman Catholic Church had come to be opposed on its central doctrine by another doctrine-driven institution, the political left, whose has slowly but surely become the ideology of the Democratic Party. Day after day, week after week, month after month, and year after year the intellectuals and activists of the Democratic Party took the party away from the central doctrines of the catechism, and hoped that the Church would follow. Although there was never any hint that Mass-attending Catholics would abandon their core beliefs, a leadership elite within the American bishops perhaps gave hope to the Democrats both with a series of thinly reasoned apologias for left-wing economics and defense policies issued in the 1980s, and in the personalities of some of the leadership, who seemed always eager to emphasize the Church's attachment to the dignity and well-being of the poor and to minimize or overlook the Church's adamant defense of the unborn.

Without pausing to see who was following them from the parish halls to the ballot boxes, confident that Mario Cuomo and Ted

Kennedy would play the Pied Pipers, the edge of the left's rhetoric moved quickly from the defense of the poor to the defense of abortion absolutism, the First Amendment–protected status of porn, and the exile of faith from the public square. By the time the left got around to extolling the justice of gay marriage—an argument announced most loudly and on a nearly constant basis by polemicist Andrew Sullivan—the Catholic faithful had stopped in their tracks and begun to look around.

Millions had thrown in with Ronald Reagan in the 1980 defeat of Jimmy Carter and again in the 1984 landslide, a hugely important pair of tradition-breaking votes for ethnic Catholics, the original "Reagan Democrats." Perhaps some had come back to the fold with Bill Clinton, and their children were certainly less likely to be with the Holy Father 100 percent of the time, though they certainly did grow up admiring the man who, along with Reagan, did the most to bring down the Soviet Union.

But they were definitely not the loyal blue-dog Democrats that some of their parents and almost all of their grandparents had been. How could they be? If they went to Mass and took seriously the Catholic catechism, the Democratic Party had long ago put itself in opposition to them.

These Catholics simply ended up at the same political place as the center-right Christians had been occupying for a hundred years: traditionalists on culture, opponents of excess, patriotic and quick to side with America in her battles overseas.

Doctrinal differences had not diminished, though years of ecumenical exchanges had taught each side how to communicate without giving instant offense to the others, with the recognition that the political elites of the left had declared war on their shared cultural attitudes. "Catholics and Evangelicals Together" was the title of a document on shared religious doctrine that emerged in the 1990s. It signaled to both banks of the orthodox Christian river that they had more in common than they had realized and enough on which they could agree politically that activism was possible.

This was a crucial development, and there is no indication that Democratic Party elites saw this huge cultural shift taking place, much less recognized the political consequence of the truce followed by the alliance. Whereas for decades Catholic Americans could expect to hear denunciation of their church originating from Protestant perspectives on Mary, the papacy, or the size of their families, now the assaults—the canon of criticism—came from a secular press guided by a secular political elite of the left, increasingly lodged in the leadership of the Democratic Party. People of faith gradually became a faction of faith, and it became obvious that when this party surfaced, it was diverse, and when it voted, it was largely Republican.

When Bill Clinton first bedded Monica Lewinsky and then lied about it, one could almost hear the Catholic ties that remained to the Democratic Party snapping. Clinton originally carried the white Catholic vote by seven points (48 to 41 percent), but after years of abortion absolutism (made most obvious in the banishment of pro-life Pennsylvania Democratic governor Bob Casey from the platform of the 1992 Democratic Convention) Clinton's degradation and its effect on the culture simply disgusted the faithful. Al Gore's smarmy rectitude did nothing to reverse it, and that's one of the chief reasons why Gore lost the white Catholic vote by seven points (45 to 52 percent) in 2000, and John Kerry lost it by thirteen points (43 to 56 percent) in 2004. That's a twenty-point swing against the Democrats, for those of you keeping track.

The Clinton degradation gave already anchored-in-the-GOP evangelicals all the more reason to double down with their political commitments. Perhaps they didn't always vote, and late-breaking scandals like George W. Bush's DUI could give the people a reason to stay home, but if they did vote, it was for the conservative candidate, and that increasingly meant the GOP candidate.

Then, of course, came the 9/11 attacks, and the awful aftermath that deepened the faithful's understanding of the world as one in which evil contended with good, where violence could arrive without warning and death without a moment's notice. When the country retreated to its churches, synagogues, and mosques, the president and all of official America gathered in the National Cathedral and prayed. Of course, hundreds of Democrats came and prayed alongside hundreds of Republicans.

As Dennis Prager says, nearly all Americans believe in God. But for those for whom the Bible is indeed God's word and not ancient man's interpretation of God's intentions, the political chasm between them and the left grew even deeper.

The next three years and three months did not give us a consistent glimpse of the hardening of political attitudes. As the prior chapter detailed, most Americans revere the American military, but the MSM and the left do not. Large majorities understand the enemy to be ruthless, but the MSM and the left do not.

Huge majorities of Americans think marriage between a man and a woman is the way it has always been and the way it should always be, but the MSM and the left do not. And vast, vast majorities of Americans think it is un-American to disqualify a fellow citizen from any sort of public service because of his or her religious beliefs or lack thereof, no matter what those beliefs are, and especially if those beliefs are simple orthodoxy.

In the next chapter, I chronicle the outline of the Democratic Party's war on the judiciary, or more specifically, those sitting judges and potential judges who are traditionalist in their approach to judging and to the moral issues on which they may be called to pass judgment.

One small skirmish in that war perfectly illustrates what has happened to the Democratic Party on the issue of religious belief. In fact, the moment the Democratic Party cast off the Catholic vote can fairly be found in the confirmation hearings of then Alabama attorney general Bill Pryor to the Eleventh Circuit Court of Appeals.

Pryor is now confirmed, with a lifetime of judicial decisions ahead of him, and perhaps even elevation to the United States Supreme Court in the future.

But instead of a routine hearing and confirmation, as would have been the case in the 200+ preceding years of Senate tradition, Democrats attacked Pryor because of his—quoting New York's Charles Schumer, one of the architects of the Dems' drive to exile religious believers from the federal bench—"deeply held beliefs."

What were those beliefs? Pryor is an orthodox, devout Roman Catholic, and holds to the Church's catechism, including the belief that human life begins at conception, and that abortion is a grave sin. All of the opposition to Pryor could be traced to this fact, and the Schumer-led assault on Pryor was a de facto declaration that devout Catholic lawyers could not be trusted on the federal bench.

Schumer's opposition to the devout and his absurd, over-the-top rhetoric directed at nominees with deep religious convictions are not limited to Catholics. During the debate on the nomination of then California supreme court justice Janice Rogers Brown to become a member of the United States Court of Appeals for the District of Columbia Circuit, Schumer histrionically asked on the floor of the Senate, "Does she want a theocracy? What does Janice Brown want to be nominated for? Dictator? Or grand exalted ruler?"[1]

"Does she want a theocracy?" sums up the hysteria of the left as it confronts a growing and broad consensus of Americans who believe that personal religious faith is not only an appropriate guide to moral issues, but also to political decisions that will affect those moral issues. Thus it has always been in the United States, but the left is driven toward a political life that would first marginalize, then exclude, and then finally stigmatize serious religious belief. Finding resistance to this program, the left cooked up the absurd charge that faith-based voters want a "theocracy," a loaded term meant to compare religious conservatives to the extremist rulers of Iran and the would-be global rulers of al Qaeda.

The attempt to scare America into voting against Republicans because of the absurd charge that their followers want a "theocracy" may be the biggest electoral mistake of the past fifty years. It is simply impossible to persuade majorities of Americans that they and their neighbors want mullah-style government because they and those neighbors oppose gay marriage or think that devout Catholics can make great judges. The deep offense given to people of faith upon being charged with extremism and kinship with the Taliban and the Iranian mullahs is sinking deeper and deeper into the consciousness of the American electorate.

It is a slander with few parallels, and the rote denials of religious bigotry when confronted with the record can not undo the deserved reputation of the left, and especially leading pundits of the left, for religious bigotry.

The unveiling of the effort to exile Catholics from the bench marked a sustained assault on people of faith that continues to this day, through this election cycle, and probably the presidential campaign of 2008.

This campaign accelerated in the spring of 2005, and it is useful to look in detail at what happened.

A chastened Democratic Party talked gamely in November and December 2004 of reconnecting with "values voters," but the election of Howard Dean as chairman of the Democratic National Committee was the worst possible move toward reconciliation with the party's roots among the religious center and old Catholic ethnic vote. James Carville and Stanley Greenberg, two of the brilliant strategists that Bill Clinton had relied upon to win the White House, devoted one of their early memos of 2005 to reconnecting with Catholics, but the election of Howard Dean was quickly followed by the tragedy of Terri Schiavo, the death of John Paul II, and the election as his successor of Benedict XVI. By the beginning of summer, it was clear that the Democratic elites could not make a serious effort at renewing their friendship with deeply religious voters, because they and their voices in the media would have none of it.

So furious did the left's punditry become in the aftermath of Congress' attempt to secure a fair hearing for Schiavo's parents that it seemed as though a collective derangement had befallen the scribblers and talking heads representing the left in the MSM.

A great summary of the collective frenzy was provided in a *Washington Post* op-ed on May 4, 2005, penned by author and former *New York Times* reporter John McCandlish Phillips. "In more than 50 years of direct engagement in and observation of the major news media I have never encountered anything remotely like the fear and loathing lavished on [evangelicals and traditional Catholics] by opinion mongers in these world-class newspapers in the past 40 days," he began. After recounting his credentials—Phillips was for eighteen years a widely admired reporter at the *New York Times*, and at the time of his hiring, the only evangelical among the paper's 275 news and editorial employees—he went on to summarize what he had seen unfold post-Schiavo:

The opening salvo of the heavy rhetorical artillery to which I object came in on March 24, when Maureen Dowd started her column in the *Times* with the declaration "Oh my God, we really are in a theocracy." While satiric, as always with the ever-soreadable columnist, it was not designed to be taken lightly. . . . Three days later Frank Rich, an often acute, broadly knowledgeable and witty cultural observer, sweepingly informed us that, under the effects of "the God racket" as now pursued in Washington, "government, culture, science, medicine, and the rule of law are all under threat from an emboldened religious minority out to remake America according to its dogma." He went on to tell *Times* readers that GOP zealots in Congress and the White House have edged our country over into "a full-scale jihad." If Rich were to have the misfortune to live for one week in a genuine jihad, and then the unlikely fortune to survive it, he would temper his categorization of the perceived President Bush–driven jihad by a minimum 77 percent. If any "emboldened minority" is aiming to "remake America according to its dogma," it seems to many evangelicals and Catholics that it is the vanguard wanting, say, the compact of marriage to be stretched in its historic definition to include men cohabitating with men and women with women. That is in terms of the history of this nation, a most pronounced and revolutionary novelty.

From March 24 through April 23 (when the [Washington] *Post* twinned Colbert I. King's "Hijacking Christianity" with Paul Gaston's "Smearing Christian Judges"), I counted 13 opinion columns of similarly alarmist tone aimed at us on the Christian right: two more in the *Post* by the generally amiable and highly communicative Richard Cohen headlined "Backward Evolution" and "Faith-Based Pandering"; one by his colleague, the urbane Eugene Robinson, "Art vs. the Church Lady" (lamenting "the pall of religiosity hanging over the city reaching gas-mask stage"); and three by Dowd, two by Paul Krugman and three by Rich in the *Times*.

In "What's Going On" [March 29], Krugman darkly implied that some committed religious believers in our nation bear a menacing resemblance to Islamic extremists, by which he did not mean a few crazed religious crackpots but a quite broad swath of red-staters. In "An Academic Question" [April 5], Krugman, conceding the wide majority of secular liberals over conservatives on the faculties of our major universities, had the chutzpah to tell us why: The former, unfettered by presuppositions of faith, are free to commit genuine investigative work and to reach valid scholarly conclusions, while the latter are disabled in that critical respect by their unproveable prior assumptions. So they are disqualified as a class from the university enterprise by their unfortunate susceptibility to the God hypothesis.

Had Phillips delayed publishing his column by a few more weeks, he could have added any number of Andrew Sullivan screeds directed at the new pope, or the characterizations by widely read leftist bloggers of American Christians as "the American Taliban," supporters of Senate Majority Leader Bill Frist as "Frist Jihadists,"[2] and Dr. James Dobson, the founder and president of Focus on the Family, as the "Ayatollah bin Dobson."[3] What can only be described as the rawest form of hate speech spewed out from the left in a volcanic eruption. Few were immune to this shudder of anti-religious bigotry. Even the estimable Christopher Hitchens wrote in the *Wall Street Journal* on May 5, 2005, of the followers of "the possibly mythical Nazarene," that they constituted "a creeping and creepy movement to impose orthodoxy on a free and pluralistic and secular Republic."

The election of Pope Benedict XVI was another occasion for the left to loudly wail about the "fundamentalism" of the religious right and especially about the backwardness of the Church of Rome. One of America's leading Catholic prelates, Archbishop Charles Chaput of

Denver, assessed the reaction to Benedict's elevation and the message the left-dominated media intended to send via the reaction:

> Benedict XVI is not only more experienced in the life of the intellect and Christian conscience than his critics, he's also more faithful to the mission of the Church and more anchored in the peace that comes from knowing and loving her founder—Jesus Christ.
>
> So the smearing begins. A *New York Times* columnist summed up the anger of the disappointed last week when she wrote that, "The white smoke (of the papal election) signaled that the Vatican thinks what it needs to bring it into modernity is the oldest pope since the 18th century: Joseph Ratzinger, a 78-year-old hidebound archconservative who ran the office that used to be called the Inquisition and who once belonged to Hitler Youth."
>
> There's an ingenious, almost elegant, dishonesty to that kind of writing. It requires real skill in misrepresenting the man and misleading the reader. It also reveals more about the columnist and the newspaper that publishes her than either might like.
>
> But they're hardly alone. Another prominent American columnist said he was "petrified" by Benedict's election. Cartoonists have had a field day over the past week engaging in anti-Church bigotry. And even our own Colorado media have repeatedly—and wrongly—described the Holy Father as a "hardliner," as if living and defending what the Catholic faith teaches is somehow fundamentalist.
>
> One of the lessons from last year that too many American Catholics still don't want to face is that it's OK to be Catholic in today's public square as long as we don't try to live our beliefs too seriously; as long as we're suitably embarrassed by all those "primitive" Catholic teachings; as long as we shut up about

abortion and other sensitive moral issues and allow ourselves to be tutored in the ways of "polite" secular culture by experts who have little or no respect for the Christian faith that guides our lives.

The reason Pope Benedict XVI will get no media honeymoon is simple. It's the same reason he instantly won the hearts of committed Catholics, worried the lukewarm and angered the proud and disaffected. He actually believes that what Jesus Christ and His Church teach is true, and that the soul of the world depends on the Church's faithful witness.[4]

"He actually believes that what Jesus Christ and His Church teach is true, and that the soul of the world depends on the Church's faithful witness"—that is a strong and accurate statement of the root cause for the left's hatred of orthodox Christian belief.

It became possible, in the spring of 2005, to say and write just about anything about religious conservatives. The *New Republic*, a venerable champion of civil liberties and American pluralism, published in its online edition an essay by Professor Ian Reifowitz that declared in its opening sentence that "the primary domestic threat to American pluralism comes from the Christian right," and which went on to argue that today's Christian conservatives reject the central project of American pluralism, "the latest in a long line of movements such as the Know-Nothing movement of the late 1840s and 1850s, the Ku Klux Klan of the 1920s, and of course the entire infrastructure of Jim Crow."

The theocratic right defines its values as the only values acceptable for true Americans and seeks to enshrine those values in law....Anyone is welcome to join adherents of the theocratic right and adopt their beliefs, but anyone who does not—gays, feminists, proponents of abortion rights, non-Christians—ultimately face second-class status in the America they plan to build.

As November 2006 approaches, expect leading Democrats to attempt to muffle this chorus of anti-religious bigotry even as they proclaim the injustice of attacks on them and their allies as anti-religious. (Indeed, in the confirmation hearings of Chief Justice John Roberts and Associate Justice Samuel Alito, the Democrats stepped carefully around the nominees' Catholic faith, aware of the perilous politics of attacks on religious belief when the national television audience is watching.) Expect to hear often of Senator Clinton's deep and sincere attachment to Methodist practice, of the Roman Catholic faithfulness of Senators Leahy, Durbin, Kerry, and Kennedy, of Senate Minority Leader Harry Reid's good standing in the Church of Jesus Christ of Latter Day Saints. Their collective tone of injury giving way to outrage is an ineffective substitute for their inaction in the face of the bigotry cited above, and it will fail to persuade any of the millions of the deeply offended who have watched the slanders roll off the tongues of the professional left for years and years.

Why did the left head down the road of anti-religious bigotry, taking the leadership elites of the Democratic Party with it? The best short answer to that enormously complicated question was provided by then Cardinal Joseph Ratzinger on the day the conclave began that would elevate him to the papacy.

"We are moving," he declared that morning, toward "a dictatorship of relativism . . . that recognizes nothing definite and leaves only one's own ego and one's own desires as the final measure."

The world, he continued, has jumped "from one extreme to the other: from Marxism to liberalism, up to libertinism; from collectivism to radical individualism; from atheism to a vague religious mysticism; from agnosticism to syncretism and on and on."

Along the way, he warned, "to have a clear faith according to the church's creed is today often labeled fundamentalism."

Nowhere is that more true than among left and liberal elites in the United States. In a culture dominated by a refusal to condemn anything as excessive and in which there is an automatic and ferocious counter-attack on any moral judgment, the abuse heaped on people with "a clear faith" was as predictable as it is intense and enduring.

Here is what happened.

First Bush won in 2000, but elites of the left and within the Democratic Party convinced themselves that this was a fluke, a stolen election.

When the elections of 2002 confirmed a strong tilt in the country to the right after 9/11, the same elites persuaded themselves that the Bush team had won by playing a "patriotism card" against victims like Max Cleland, and that the armies of common sense would rise up to throw out the Halliburton clique in November 2004.

When the opposite occurred, and the outlines of the Bush realignment and mandate finally became so clear as to be undeniable, the same elites simply panicked and began lashing out, once again telling themselves a comforting story about election fraud in Ohio and hoping that fear-mongering about "theocrats" could bring the country back toward their candidates and platforms when in fact their tactics have exactly the opposite effect.

The Democratic Party has become a party dedicated to religious bigotry. Read any of the leading leftist bloggers, study the speeches of Senator Schumer and his colleagues opposing judicial nominee after judicial nominee, and simply listen to Democrats talk on Air America or any of a dozen cable shows. They cannot stop themselves from hating the religious right, yet the religious right they have in mind is vast beyond counting, and includes what used to be core Democratic constituencies.

In fact, as African American pastor after African American pastor begins to consider the issue set in front of him and by extension his congregation, the stress on the most vital of all Democratic constituencies grows higher and higher. The black church is a fundamentalist church, even as it embraces the social gospel. It has never before been forced to abandon its Democratic Party allies, but on issue after issue that is exactly the choice being forced on these pastors and congregations.

Americans who believe in God and in the divine origin of the Bible and its inerrancy are being pushed out of the Democratic Party, even if the Democratic Party doesn't know it is doing the pushing. A majority party could only indulge such indifference at its peril. For a minority party—and make no mistake, the Dems are now the minority party in this country—such indifference is suicidal.

The anti-traditional religious pressure is so great within the Democratic Party, though, that it cannot be contained or even disguised. In early June 2005, Howard Dean said about Republicans, "They all behave the same. They all look the same. It's pretty much a white Christian party."

The shocked Democratic elite quickly tried to distance itself from Dean. Why? In the words of hard-left blogger "Billmon," writing at his blog, The Whiskey Bar[5], "gratuitously alienating white Christian voters is pretty high on my political not-to-do list," even as he admitted that within the Democratic Party "lefty analysts dream of a future in which a coalition of non-whites and non-Christian whites can carry the day in this country."

Why is the hostility to the religious voter growing? Because it has become apparent in setting after setting that those religious voters are saying: "this far and no farther."

They could accommodate themselves to "choice," but not to late-term abortion and the exile of parents from the decisions of their minor children. They could welcome and embrace full civil rights and the vigorous protection of the laws for gays and lesbians, but they do not think it is discrimination to limit marriage to one man and one woman, and while they refuse to involve themselves in the bedrooms of their neighbors, neither are they indifferent to a public culture increasingly tawdry and degraded.

They think a vibrant faith life is to be celebrated, not mocked. They are proud and tolerant Americans, not mullahs with Kalashnikovs, and they deeply resent the imputation to the contrary on the lips of every liberal pundit standing in for the Democratic Party in print or on the airwaves.

In short, the left pushed too far, and did so via edict, not election, relying on courts and mayors like San Francisco's Gavin Newsom to simply declare a cultural hegemony.

And that is not a situation ordinary Americans of ordinary religious beliefs are going to put up with. In fact, the massive shift toward W in November 2004 was just the beginning. Lefty blogger and former Howard Dean campaign consultant Chris Bowers, writing at his blog, MyDD[6], summarized the trend:

> The quickest way to summarize the developing demographic trends of the two coalitions is a white Christian coalition versus a non-white and/or non-Christian coalition. The voting habits of non-whites and white non-Christians are rapidly approaching parity, just as the voting of white Protestants and white Catholics are doing the same. Further, race and religion are now far better at determining how someone will vote than region, income, union membership, or pretty much anything else you could name.

Although I hope it does not happen and we should work to make sure it does not happen, as time goes on I fully expect that white Catholics will continue their Republican trend until their voting habits are nearly indistinguishable from those of white Protestants (who are also turning sharply Republican).

The indifference-turned-to-hostility toward people with traditional religious views is the simple result of the abandonment of the hard-left Democrats by those people. The left isn't interesting in winning them back, as that would require abandoning their hard-won policy domination of the Democratic Party.

And they can't simply be allowed to leave—they have to be demonized on their way out the door.

The second crucial message of Election 2006 is that the Democratic Party has allowed itself to be infected by a virulent strain of anti-religious bigotry that, if unchecked, would result in the very anti-pluralistic strictures it warns about in a made-up "theocratic right." The viciousness of the left's rhetoric on anything having to do with religious belief is a heartfelt hatred of the belief systems of mainstream Protestants and Catholics, and the drive to block from the bench nominees of ordinary orthodoxy is a foreshadowing of the place in public life that left-dominated government would grant to the ordinary orthodox—that is to say, none.

Again, the left and the MSM will howl and howl again when any of its members hears this message; but the record is in black and white, the evidence is clear, and only a few of the thousands of possible examples are reproduced above.

The key is to make sure your neighbors know about it in detail. They already suspect it, of course, and any person reasonably familiar with American media has heard the familiar refrains of anti-religious bigotry enough times to immediately recognize the pattern and its practitioners.

The upshot has to be increased political activity by the ordinary orthodox, and the continued development of alternative, unbiased media to communicate with them.

One of the reasons I am so enthusiastic about the rise of the blogosphere is because it finally provided the means for ordinary orthodox Americans to communicate with each other free of the disfiguring filter of MSM. Overnight, an archipelago of blogs and web sites devoted to living the Christian life were formed, and some of them directly targeted the political implications of Christian belief.

Pastors long afraid of violating the tax laws of the United States by veering too close to politics, leadership fearful of receiving an incendiary and threatening letter from one of the left's anti-religious crusaders such as Barry Lynn of Americans United for Separation of Church and State, can now safely set up their own blog under their own name and exercise their own First Amendment right to political speech, right down to the specific suggestion of the best candidate for office at every level.

Superb essayists on politics and morality and theology can now publish at almost no cost and can debate at almost endless length any mater of public interest. Go to Google and enter the names EvangelicalOutpost.com, MarkDRoberts.com, John Mark Reynolds, Albert Mohler, or any of the literally thousands of superb faith-based bloggers and the information explosion will become obvious immediately.

When John McCandlish Phillips began his career as a *New York Times* reporter, he was the only evangelical among a vast legion of writers and reporters. Not much has changed in the newsrooms and television and radio studios of America; in fact, those media types have gone further left in the past two decades, and are even more reliably Democratic in their biases and more hostile to the ordinary orthodox.

But it hardly matters at all. New media arrived almost overnight, and the ordinary orthodox can get news and analysis from trustworthy sources not hostile from the get-go to their worldview, and who share at least in part their understanding of the importance of Scripture and morals.

Again, none of the names I have given are other than complete "liberals" when it comes to robust religious freedom and separation of church and state. Like me, they are center-right believers in the genius of the founders and the importance of religious pluralism, even as each names Christ as Savior and Lord.

Together with them and their thousands of other pastors and priests and rabbis and, yes, imams and monks, para-chruch workers, lay leaders and simple congregants, the ordinary orthodox are slowly but surely making a political home in the Republican Party because that party is committed to the traditional morality that permeates all of their faith traditions. They recognize the truth of the second message: the Democratic left has rejected their deeply held faith and the moral values based on their beliefs.

That migration will accelerate as this message spreads. So spread it.

CHAPTER FIVE

GOP MESSAGE 3

The Democratic Left and Its Senators Have Declared War on the Judiciary

This isn't complicated. Democrats have discovered that their politics make it very difficult for them to win enough elections to put together majorities in either the United States Senate or the House of Representatives.

They have also discovered that the presidency isn't their calling either. The last time a Democratic candidate for president won a pure majority of the popular vote was 1976, and Jimmy Carter's 50.1 percent of the vote was hardly a staggering win. Clinton's 42.93 percent in 1992 and 49.24 percent in 1996, as well as Al Gore's 48.4 percent in 2000 and John Kerry's 48.27 percent in 2004, underscore the fact that a real ceiling limits any Democratic nominee's reach.

And that ceiling is dropping as populations shift dramatically to southern and western states in a trend that will continue over the next thirty years, according to Census Bureau projections. "The net beneficiary of this will continue to be the Republican Party because the population shift is moving into an environment that is heavily dominated by Republicans," according to Emory University professor Merle Black, an expert in demographics and politics. With the population of the South projected to grow by more than 40 percent, and the West's by more than 45 percent, the advantage for the GOP is simply huge. (The population of the Midwest is targeted to drop 9.5 percent and the Northeast's by 7.6 percent.)

With the Congress beyond their reach and the presidency more than likely to land in Republican hands, Democrats have figured out that their long-term access to power is via the federal courts. If they can pack the courts with liberal activist judges while blocking conservative judges during the long stretches of GOP control of the White House, they can hope to legislate their policy objectives from the bench.

"A majority vote of nine unelected judges" is how Justice Antonin Scalia has referred to high court rulings that sweep away the legislative judgments of elected majorities at both the federal and state levels. And, truth be told, that is all the Democrats can hope for in the next generation of American politics—a robustly activist and liberal-dominated Supreme Court combined with long life for the Clinton appointees on the lower courts, as well as ascendancy of left-dominated state supreme courts.

Although this reality is now quite obvious to even the densest Democrat with an understanding of the numbers and demographics set out on the political table, it probably wasn't what motivated the original assault on the federal judiciary, which began with the nomination of Judge Robert Bork to the Supreme Court in 1987.

Bork was a distinguished judge on the United States Court of Appeals for the District of Columbia Circuit and a widely respected legal scholar, as well as former solicitor general of the United States, when Ronald Reagan nominated him to join the highest court. But within an hour of the announcement, Ted Kennedy had gone to the Senate floor to denounce Bork in the harsh terms that set the standard for the twenty years of ferocious attacks on Republican nominees that have followed. Kennedy exclaimed at one point:

> Robert Bork's America is a land in which women would be forced into back-alley abortions, blacks would sit at segregated lunch counters, rogue police could break down citizens' doors in midnight raids, schoolchildren could not be taught about evolution, writers and artists could be censored at the whim of government, and the doors of the federal courts would be shut on the fingers of millions of citizens.

The Bork nomination then melted down as the left turned on flame-thrower after flame-thrower. The Republicans were simply unprepared for such tactics. One account summarizes the timeline of the event:

> As Bork's September 15 confirmation hearing approached, liberal and conservative pressure groups spent an unprecedented $20 million in campaigns to either demonize or praise the candidate. The AFL-CIO, the American Civil Liberties Union, Common Cause, the NAACP, and the National Organization of Women were just a few of the organizations that hurled themselves into the fray in order to prevent Bork's ascension to the highest court in the land. They argued that the Ninth Amendment, which states that the "enumeration . . . of

certain rights" in the Constitution "shall not be construed to deny or disparage others retained by the people," justified judicial activism. In other words, the Constitution acknowledged unidentified rights and it was up to the Supreme Court to define and defend them in keeping with the premise that Americans should live in a free society where all people were equally protected under the law. Bork's opinions and writings, said his critics, revealed a man who posed a serious threat to basic principles of social justice.

The American public gave mixed signals when polled about the Bork controversy. A Gallup poll on the eve of the confirmation hearings revealed that two out of three could not even name Reagan's candidate for the Supreme Court. By a 52 to 40 percent margin, those polled agreed with the concept of judicial restraint in accordance with the "original intent" of the Constitution, but at the same time favored by a 52 to 42 percent spread the Supreme Court's decision to allow a woman to end a pregnancy—a right nowhere enunciated in the Constitution.

Among the fourteen members of the Judiciary Committee, Biden, Kennedy, Howard Metzenbaum (D-OH), and Paul Simon (D-IL) were staunchly opposed to Bork's nomination while Strom Thurmond (R-SC) and Orrin Hatch (R-UT) were his most fervent supporters. The swing votes appeared to rest with Democrats Howell Heflin of Alabama and Dennis DeConcini of Arizona as well as with Republican Arlen Specter of Pennsylvania. There were many who felt Bork's erudition and quick wit made him more than a match for the legislators who would question him.

In his five days of testimony—the longest confirmation hearing for any Supreme Court nominee since hearings began in 1939—Bork surprised everyone. He modified many of his most controversial views. Whereas in 1971 he had argued that constitutional protection of free speech applied only to that which was political in nature, in 1987 he conceded that First Amendment guarantees applied to news, opinion, literature, and more. He had claimed that the "equal protection" clause of the Fourteenth Amendment should apply only to racial and not gender discrimination; during the hearing he stated that equal protection should in fact apply also to women. Bork's approach to the hearing was in keeping with the decision by the White House to avoid an ideological fight and tout the nominee as a moderate. This soft sell did not sit well with Bork's supporters, his detractors, or the undecided senators.

Another week of testimony by a hundred witnesses followed Bork's appearance. Among them was William T. Coleman, a prominent black Republican attorney and a strong supporter of Reagan. But Coleman broke ranks with the president this time, speaking out in opposition to confirmation. "When it has counted," he wrote in a *New York Times* op-ed piece, "Robert Bork has often stood against the aspirations of blacks to achieve their constitutional rights." Former Texas congresswoman Barbara Jordan and Atlanta mayor Andrew Young also testified against the nominee. When Senators Specter, Heflin, and DeConcini joined the anti-Bork contingent of the Judiciary Committee, the White House hinged its hopes on the full Senate's vote. The Democrats had regained control of the Senate by a 54 to 46 margin in the 1986 elections, so Reagan counted on the conservative southern Democrats who had supported his tax and budget cuts to save the day for Bork. But polls showed that a majority of southern whites opposed Bork, so the Democratic senators from the South faced no political backlash at home by voting against confirmation.

On October 6, the Judiciary Committee voted 9 to 5 against confirming Bork and most of the judge's supporters, realizing that a full vote in the Senate would also go against their man, expected Bork to withdraw from the process. But Bork announced he would continue the fight, though he was disappointed by waning support from the White House. "A crucial principle is at stake," he said, articulating his view that the selection process should not be corrupted by "campaigns of distortion" like the one being waged against him. On October 23, the Senate voted 58 to 42 against the nomination.[1]

Whatever works is what you get until it stops working. The Democrats had demolished a nomination by resort to the worst sort of demagoguery. They would not unlearn that lesson. They have not unlearned it yet.

Republicans, on the other hand, disdained such tactics on Supreme Court nominees, though they too have endeavored to put their mark on the courts, even while President Clinton was in office. The result has been a steadily growing face-off over nominees, with every president since Carter seeing a lower percentage of his nominees confirmed. Mathematician John Daly did the math and came up with some highly instructive tables.[2]

Congress	President	Nominated	Confirmed	Withdrawn	Returned	Rejected	Senate Composition
79th	Truman	8	7	1	0	0	56D 38R
80th	Truman	3	3	0	0	0	51R 45D
81st	Truman	20	15	0	5	0	54D 42R
82nd	Truman	2	2	0	0	0	49D 47R
79th–82nd	**Truman**	**33**	**27**	**1**	**5**	**0**	
83rd	Eisenhower	13	12	0	1	0	48R 47D
84th	Eisenhower	13	11	0	2	0	48D 47R
85th	Eisenhower	12	11	0	1	0	49D 47R
86th	Eisenhower	13	12	0	1	0	65D 35R
83rd–86th	**Eisenhower**	**51**	**46**	**0**	**5**	**0**	
87th	Kennedy	22	17	0	5	0	65D 35R
88th	Kennedy/ Johnson	7	7	0	0	0	67D 33R
89th	Johnson	26	25	0	1	0	68D 32R
90th	Johnson	13	12	0	1	0	64D 36R
87th–90th	**Kennedy/ Johnson**	**68**	**61**	**0**	**7**	**0**	
91st	Nixon	23	20	2	1	0	57D 43R
92nd	Nixon	18	18	0	0	0	54D 44R
93rd	Nixon/Ford	13	10	0	3	0	56D 42R
94th	Ford	11	9	0	2	0	60D 37R
91st–94th	**Nixon/Ford**	**65**	**57**	**2**	**6**	**0**	
95th	Carter	12	12	0	0	0	61D 38R
96th	Carter	49	44	1	4	0	58D 41R
95th–96th	**Carter**	**61**	**56**	**1**	**4**	**0**	

Congress	President	Nominated	Confirmed	Withdrawn	Returned	Rejected	Senate Composition
97th	Reagan	20	19	0	1	0	53R 46D 1I
98th	Reagan	22	14	1	7	0	55R 45D
99th	Reagan	34	33	0	1	0	53R 47D
100th	Reagan	26	17	2	7	0	55D 45R
97th–100th	**Reagan**	**102**	**83**	**3**	**16**	**0**	
101st	G.H.W. Bush	23	22	0	1	0	54D 46R
102nd	G.H.W. Bush	31	20	0	11	0	56D 44R
101st–102nd	**G.H.W. Bush**	**54**	**42**	**0**	**12**	**0**	
103rd	Clinton	22	19	0	3	0	57D 43R
104th	Clinton	20	11	1	8	0	52R 48D
105th	Clinton	30	20	1	9	0	55R 45D
106th	Clinton	34	15	1	18	0	55R 45D
103rd–106th	**Clinton**	**106**	**65**	**3**	**38**	**0**	
107th	G.W. Bush	32	17	0	15	0	D50 R49 1I
108th	G.W. Bush	34	18	1	16	0	R51 D48 1I
107th–108th	**G.W. Bush**	**66**	**35**	**1**	**31**	**0**	

And this one:

President	Confirmation Percentage
Truman	81.8%
Eisenhower	90.2%
Kennedy/Johnson	89.7%
Nixon/Ford	89.1%
Carter	91.8%
Reagan	81.3%
G.H.W. Bush	77.8%
Clinton	61.3%
G.W. Bush	53.0%

And this one compares confirmation success of a new president's nominees in his first two years in office, including his so-called "honeymoon" year:

President	Confirmation Percentage 1st Congress
Truman	87.5%
Eisenhower	92.3%
Kennedy	77.2%
Johnson	100.0%
Nixon	87.0%
Ford	76.9%
Carter	100.0%
Reagan	95.0%
G.H.W. Bush	95.6%
Clinton	86.3%
G.W. Bush	53.1%

And finally, this one compares the presidents' first-term success in putting judges onto the federal appeals courts.

President	Confirmation Percentage 1st and 2nd Congress
Truman	90.9%
Eisenhower	88.5%
Johnson	97.0%
Nixon	92.7%
Ford	79.2%
Carter	91.8%
Reagan	78.6%
G.H.W. Bush	77.8%
Clinton	71.4%
G.W. Bush	52.2%

What Daly's statistics demonstrate conclusively is this: from 1987 and the Bork nomination through the showdown over the issue in the spring and summer of 2005, the Democrats consistently upped the effort to control and politicize the judicial selection process, and succeeded in bringing the process to its lowest point ever.

In the aftermath of a crushing defeat in Senate elections in 2004, when the GOP picked up a net of four seats in the Senate, the Democrats refused to abandon their obstructionism on the issue of judicial nominations. They continued to employ filibusters—the refusal to end debate—in order to prevent up or down votes on nominees they knew would have majority support in the Senate. The Senate Republicans moved slowly in response, eventually preparing to employ a parliamentary device first invented by Democrat Robert Byrd of Virginia when he was the Senate's majority leader.

Called the "nuclear option" by Trent Lott, the "constitutional option" by Bill Frist, and "the Byrd option" by others, this maneuver would put to the presiding officer of the Senate—the vice president of the United States, Dick Cheney—the question of whether a filibuster was appropriate conduct under the rules of the Senate in the consideration of nominees to the federal appeals court.

On only one occasion, in the previous century, a filibuster had been used against a nominee to the Supreme Court. When Chief Justice Earl Warren retired in 1968, Lyndon Johnson attempted to elevate his friend (some would say Johnson's crony) Abe Fortas from his position as associate justice on the Supreme Court to that of chief justice. When hearings revealed Fortas's highly inappropriate conduct on the bench and his clearly questionable ethics, resistance grew to the idea of a lame duck president saddling the Supreme Court of the United States with an ethically challenged leader. When the Fortas nomination came before the Senate for a vote in early October—a month before the showdown between Richard Nixon and Hubert Humphrey at the polls—the Senate refused to close debate as a signal to LBJ that if a vote were held, his friend might suffer the embarrassment of a defeat. No second push for a vote was held, the Fortas nomination was withdrawn, and Fortas later resigned from the Court.

This extraordinary circumstance was the only time a filibuster had ever been used against a Supreme Court nominee in the one hundred years prior to the Democrats' embrace of obstruction in the aftermath of their loss of the Senate in the November 2003 elections. Despite their punishment at the polls, the Democrats began employing filibuster after filibuster against highly qualified judicial nominees for the appeals court, trashing reputations as well as precedents as they went over the left edge of the cliff under the leadership of Tom Daschle, Patrick Leahy, Ted Kennedy, and Charles Schumer.

The shortsighted Democrats handed President Bush and the GOP a stick to beat them with throughout the next political cycle, and beaten they were—soundly, and not just in the presidential polling. Daschle was tossed from office, and the big swing toward GOP control of the Senate chamber continued.

It was astonishing on a political level for the Democrats to consult their losses and conclude that their new strategy in 2005 would be even more of the obstructionism that had brought them ruin in 2002 and 2004—but that is exactly what happened. So radicalized had the Democratic activist base become under the influence of MoveOn.Org, Howard Dean, and Michael Moore that the elected senators could not take their party back. The self-destructive left demanded more self-destruction.

As the nuclear option came close to deployment in the spring of 2005, a handful of Democratic senators looked for a face-saving compromise, and a handful of Republican faint-hearts obliged. The so-called "Gang of 14" huddled in the days before the appeal to the Senate chair and announced a "deal" had been reached, thanks primarily to the good offices of Senator John McCain.

Some explanation is in order. McCain—who ought always to be described first as a great American and then as a lousy senator and a terrible Republican—seemed to have been driven in these negotiations by a need to avoid voting against the ruling of the chair. He quite unexpectedly announced this in response to a question from Chris Matthews on an edition of *Hardball*. McCain had dodged and dodged question after question on the maneuver, as did the other Senate GOP maverick, Nebraska's Chuck Hagel. But his sudden declaration to Matthews that he would not vote with the GOP on this crucial issue unleashed a gale of criticism within the party.

McCain had spent four years repairing the damage his explosive temper unleashed in the aftermath of his primary loss, patiently and energetically appearing for candidates across the country and working hard to secure the re-election of George W. Bush. But this mistake was fatal to his still very much alive presidential ambitions. To be the party's nominee, you must be strong on defense, committed to low taxes, pro-life, and reliable on the issue of judicial appointees. McCain's stunning refusal to bring constitutional order and fair play back to the confirmation process put not a scarlet letter but a scarlet sentence on McCain: he can't be trusted to put the cause of good judges ahead of political gain.

Whether McCain was bolting the GOP because of his professed belief in Senate prerogative, or because he thought siding with the noisy media and the Dems against the new GOP majority would enhance his reputation with the chattering class, we can't know. But overnight he went from nearly rehabilitated GOP presidential nomination contender to being best described as "through," even by some of his loyal fans.

One example: throughout the primaries of 2000 I would argue the Bush side of the Bush-McCain contest with my longtime and very close friend Joseph Timothy Cook, an occasional guest host for me on the program, a retired plaintiffs' lawyer in airline disaster litigation, and crucially a Naval Academy graduate and Vietnam-era pilot who flew bombing runs over Vietnam and had briefly served in the same squadron as McCain. Cook had contributed the max to the Arizona senator's presidential drive that year. Most of our conversations were heated and a few were even angry, because we both were passionate about our preference.

The day McCain announced his decision to vote against the Republicans on judges, Cook stopped by my studio to tell me he was finished with McCain, and that he had sent an e-mail to his office to that effect. I suspect that McCain heard from thousands and maybe tens of thousands of Cooks.

I also suspect that as the political damage he had done to himself was assessed, McCain hit upon the plan that led to the "compromise": he had to find a way to avoid voting against the constitutional option, and if possible, of voting for it. Thus the vaguely worded compromise that allowed all but two of George W. Bush's appellate nominees to move forward with a guarantee that seven Democratic senators would join with Republicans to assure floor votes for every judicial nominee unless "extraordinary circumstances" arose. With a radicalized base, the Dems will not be able to hold to this commitment, and when they break it, McCain—no doubt more in sorrow than in anger—will have an excuse for voting for the chair's ruling that ought to have been his first position, given that all arguments for or against the filibuster will be exactly as they were in April 2005. There will be no changed circumstance from the day McCain announced to Chris Matthews that he was against curtailing the filibuster powers of the Senate minority. Most of the MSM will have missed this crucial issue, but not the base.

A truce in the judiciary wars brought about by the "compromise" did not last the summer. The announcement of John Roberts's nomination was only hours old when Nan Aron, Ralph Neas, and other battle-hardened veterans of the left who have been waging war in the judiciary since the Bork nomination were out in force denouncing it. This very important revelation will be a major issue in the coming months, even though Roberts and Alito were easily confirmed.

It is important because it shows that the left cannot accept even phenomenally qualified justices if they are conservative. Justice Roberts and I were colleagues in the Reagan White House Counsel's office for a year, as well as teammates on a White House basketball team and relay team, "Reagan's V-toes," which ran in the Nike Capitol Challenge. I haven't spoken much with him in the twenty years since, but I can echo what people quite familiar with his later work testified to immediately after his nomination and throughout the confirmation process: he is the most talented lawyer with whom I have ever worked, and a splendid human being of first-rate character.

Yet the left attacked him from the first day forward. No matter how many testified to his judicial temperament and extraordinary abilities, as well as his fundamental decency, still the left attacked and attacked and attacked. Because he was not one of them, he was a target, and the attacks were as repellant as they were ineffective. The *New York Times* even probed the circumstances of his childrens' adoptions, and only the instant and nearly complete disgust of the vast majority of Americans forced a pledge from the *Times* that nothing inappropriate would be pursued—a shameful admission that inquiries had indeed been made on the subject.

Then the National Abortion Rights Action League ran a television spot that was intended to deceive viewers into believing that Roberts had defended abortion clinic bombers. Again outrage across the spectrum of decent Americans forced a retreat. The mask was off the left again, and a disbelieving center was confronted with more evidence of its relentlessness and irrational fury.

Always the left overreaches, and each time more and more Americans come to the conclusion that not only does this alliance of arch-liberals dominating the Democrats have bad ideas, they have bad intentions and worse ethics. The judges debate will revive with every new outrageous decision from the bench, whether the decision of a federal district court judge in Washington state to sentence the would-be murderer of hundreds, if not thousands, of Americans at LAX on New Year's Eve 1999 to a sentence of effectively fourteen more years from the date of sentencing in the summer of 2005, or the Supreme court's consulting of foreign law to overturn legislated conclusions on the appropriate age and circumstance of death penalties, or the same Court's approval of the condemning of one man's house to build another man's mall. The judiciary branch has forfeited a great deal of the public's trust, in large part because the courts have seized a great deal of the public's power through the decisions of the left's representatives on the federal and state benches.

Twenty-two Democratic senators voted against Chief Justice Roberts's confirmation—an astonishing and almost hilarious admission that for the hard-left wing of the Democratic Party, no nominee not sent forward by a Democratic president is acceptable to them. The opposition to the next nominee, Samuel Alito, took on the same otherworldly quality as extremist after extremist lined up to explain how this model jurist with fifteen years' experience on the circuit court and past service as United States Attorney and associate solicitor general was not fit to serve on the Supreme Court. Even more jaw-dropping arguments followed, as Democratic senators struggled to dress up abortion right absolutism as other than that. The candor was lacking, but not clarity.

And so it will remain for the foreseeable future. Every nominee to the Supreme Court, and probably most to the circuit courts of appeal, will be automatically opposed by the hard left of the Democratic Party, and their allies in MSM and left-wing interest groups. This underscores the importance of the Senate elections of 2006, given the advanced age of many members of the current court.

The lesson of the fall of 2005 is that this opposition must be confronted frontally, and not via "stealth nominees."

When Chief Justice Rehnquist died, President Bush quickly announced that his nominee for the vacancy created by the retirement of Sandra Day O'Connor, John Roberts, would become his nominee for the vacancy left by Rehnquist's passing. Shortly after Roberts's confirmation, Bush announced his nomination of White House Counsel Harriet Miers to fill the O'Connor seat. A firestorm of criticism, much of it unfair and unfounded, exploded on the right. Amid repeated allegations that Miers lacked the intellectual capacity to do the job, the White House found a way to withdraw the nomination based on the looming confrontation with some senators over the confidentiality of opinions given by Miers to the president in her capacity as a White House lawyer. (This cover story deserves the title of the Krauthammer Option, as it was first suggested in print by columnist Charles Krauthammer.)

I was a vigorous defender of the Miers nomination once it was announced, even though my preference for either Judge Michael Luttig of the Fourth Circuit Court of Appeals or Judge Michael McConnell of the Tenth Circuit had been frequently and forcefully argued in many forums. My view was and remains that the president knew Harriet Miers so well that his judgment on her judicial philosophy was trustworthy. The Framers never intended the Supreme Court to become what it has now morphed into: a sort of judicial monastery limited only to long-serving Supreme Court parishioners of one sort or another—appellate judges, veterans of the solicitor general's office, or academics specializing in constitutional law.

But that debate is over, and while its costs have not yet been tallied—it will take a few years of decisions from Justice Alito and a few rounds of confirmation battles yet to be fought to assess the fallout from the Miers nomination and withdrawal—the immediate consequence is clear. Supreme Court nominees from Republican presidents will always be opposed by the left and their kept senators in the Democratic caucus, and will not earn the support of many conservatives among the right's interest groups, unless there is a pedigree of the sort that Roberts and Alito brought with them.

This means that, like some of the battlefields of the Civil War, the same ground in the war for the judiciary will be fought over again and again, each time with the outcome in doubt and the stakes incredibly high. With President Bush's stamp on the Supreme Court and appellate courts now so distinct, the despair among the left is verging on desperation, and the remaining pockets of judicial activists— the Ninth Circuit Court of Appeals, which sees in the Pledge of Allegiance's invocation of "under God" an unconstitutional "establishment of religion," for example, or the Massachusetts Supreme Court, home of the imperial judiciary's first diktat concerning same-sex marriage—will become even more bold.

The good news is that each desperate overreach underscores with particular vigor just how far the Democrat elites have strayed from the American mainstream.

It is crucial to understand the source of the left's panic as it surveys the progress President Bush has made in restoring the federal courts to their constitutional role. Not only does that understanding prepare the center-right for the future battles, it illuminates the left's world view in a stark and undeniable fashion.

When the confirmation of Judge Alito became a near certainty, the Nans, Kates, and Ralphs began bellowing "Here There Be Monsters" as they issued dire warning after dire warning of the direction the remade SCOTUS would take.

But they knew, as did all the senators and most serious Court watchers, that there was no imminent threat to *Casey/Roe*, even if Chief Justice Roberts and soon-to-be-Justice Alito joined in a bloc with Justices Scalia and Thomas. Even if Justice Kennedy were to change his view and join in consigning the Roe Era to the same bin of history as the Lochner Era, access to abortion would remain as the law of the land throughout most of the land.

Despite this, the left is now genuinely panicked, and it is interesting to focus on the source of that panic. Its roots are in a greatly oversimplified view of the individual justices' beliefs and a vastly understated complexity of the Court's work, but it is a real panic nonetheless.

The four-square box to the right is not intended to represent accurately or even closely the real views of the justices. Rather, it does represent the left's beliefs about the beliefs of the justices.

By "theist" I mean those who hold a belief in a God who is not indifferent to the actions of men and women. "Secularists," by contrast, believe that the existence of such a God is, at best, unknowable.

"Constitutional majoritarians" are believers in checks and balances and separation of powers and the federal system, but also are subscribers to the view that majorities working through representative institutions must ultimately control the direction of the country, bound only by the Constitution's directives.

"Elitist anti-majoritarians," by contrast, believe that no matter what popular opinion expressed through representative institutions may believe, that there are certain policy choices that must be imposed on the country, even if there is no clear constitutional backing for such a choice, and even if that choice has no history of legislative consent. In recent years, elitist anti-majoritarians have, for example, been committed to the abolition of the death penalty and for the imposition of same-sex marriage, but they have many other policy preferences as well.

Many of the left's opinion leaders are secular, elitist anti-majoritarians. Many more, while holding a sincere belief in God, are so committed to the idea of a public square empty of God that their political choices are indistinguishable from those of avowed secularists who reject the very idea of God.

Here's how the left understands the direction of the SCOTUS:

	Theists	Secularists
Constitutional Majoritarians	Scalia Thomas Alito Roberts	Rehnquist O'Connor
Elitist Anti-Majoritarians	Kennedy	Stevens Breyer Souter Ginsburg

The real fear on the left is not so much the possibility that a bloc is forming that will vote the wrong way, but that this bloc will raise arguments that are persuasive far beyond the narrow decisions the justices are called upon to render.

In recent years, it has been very rare for a majority or even a plurality of SCOTUS to speak the language of traditional morality. (For an example of such language, see Justice Scalia's dissent in *Stenberg v. Carhart*, the case in which five justices upheld the barbaric practice of partial-birth abortion, which Scalia denounced in stark and deserved terms.)

The majority decisions of recent years applauded by conservatives, such as *Lopez* and *Morrison*, have honored the values of constitutional majoritarians, but they are not the sort of decisions that employ arguments from a theist worldview, and they are far less troubling to the left than would be a majority-backed Scalia opinion on the subject of, say, partial-birth abortion or a majority-backed Thomas opinion on the evils of race-consciousness in college admissions.

If a bloc of four justices does emerge that begins to speak in the language of constitutional majoritarianism and traditional, theist morality, it will represent the launch of an entirely new class of legal battleship which, with the assistance of new media, will have a range never before seen when it comes to arguing about the course of constitutional law. Further, that range will extend far beyond the legal debates before the courts. Persuasive arguments are very potent things.

It isn't just the prospect of the decisions themselves that so alarms the left, I think, but also their fear of being totally and completely routed when it comes to persuasive argument.

The trumped-up charge that a new SCOTUS majority will go hunting for occasions on which to impose their natural law–driven jurisprudence is absurd. But the prospect of tightly argued opinions in defense of majoritarian choices within our constitutional frame-work, which honor the traditional morality of the vast majority of Americans, well, that is something to look forward to. That is, if you are not a member of an elite who is certain that your views, while not widely shared, are nevertheless preferable to those of the unwashed masses.

The elitist anti-majoritarians will be losing sleep as they lose their last bastion of power, and their actions will only reinforce our mes-sage: that the Democratic left has declared war on the judiciary.

Now these elites will have to win elections if they want to make policy, and that's a daunting prospect indeed, especially if they are committed to the imposition of extraordinarily unpopular schemes of the worst sort of social engineering, such as same-sex marriage.

CHAPTER SIX

GOP MESSAGE 4

The Democratic Left Wants to Radically Redefine Marriage While Portraying Republicans as Bigoted

There are many books on the issue of whether men should be able to marry men and women should be able to marry women. They are often well argued and certainly passionate. But none of them have been persuasive on public opinion.

Every time the issue of same-sex marriage is put to the people, the people vote overwhelmingly to preserve marriage as an institution uniquely intended to exist between one man and one woman. The one federal statute on the subject, the Defense of Marriage Act, was signed by Bill Clinton into law on September 21, 1996, after passing both the House and the Senate by overwhelming majorities. "DOMA," as the act is called, defines marriage as a "legal union between one man and one woman as husband and wife" and defined a spouse as a "person of the opposite sex who is a husband or a wife." DOMA affected the more than 1,000 laws that determine eligibility for federal benefits, rights, or privileges. It was also intended to prevent the export from one state to another of same-sex marriages and the recognition of same-sex marriages performed abroad in countries that either had allowed it or are on the brink of allowing it.

Some states have legislated same-sex partnership laws. Hawaii did so in May 1997. Vermont did so in December 1999, under pressure from the state supreme court. In September 2003, California's legislature passed, and about-to-be recalled governor Gray Davis signed, a sweeping domestic partnership law that provided same-sex civil unions with almost the identical status of married couples, without actually using the term marriage.

Two months later, on November 18, the Massachusetts Supreme Judicial Council, in a 4–3 ruling, held, in the words of the *New York Times*, "that gays have the right to marry under the state constitution, emphatically stating that the Commonwealth had failed to identify any constitutional reasons why same-sex couples could not wed."

Not long after this decision, grandstanding local elected officials seeking national visibility or the approval of their local constituencies ordered other local officials to issue marriage licenses to same sex couples in San Francisco, California; New Paltz, New York; Kings County in Washington state; and other places.

A counter-movement gathered momentum, and President Bush announced support for an amendment to the United States Constitution that would limit marriage to the union of one man and one woman. Stuck in a politically difficult position, every candidate for the Democratic presidential nomination rejected the idea of same-sex marriage but also opposed the constitutional amendment supported by Bush.

By mid-March, a *New York Times*/CBS poll found solid majorities against same-sex marriage and against the proposed amendment: "By 59 percent to 35 percent, respondents said they supported a constitutional amendment that would 'allow marriage only between a man and a woman.' But 56 percent said that they did not view the issue as important enough to merit changing the nation's constitution. 'It seems like a waste of time and energy when we should be thinking about figuring out how we're going to have Social Security,' said Ronald Sharp, 44, a Republican and retired mental health care aide from Detroit."[1]

The polls that counted began to arrive on September 18, when Louisiana voters overwhelmingly approved a state constitutional amendment banning not only same-sex marriages but also civil unions along the California model. Although the House of Representatives voted 277–186 in favor of the constitutional amendment, that total was 49 votes short of the necessary super-majority to put the issue to the states, and the Senate refused to even take up the issue, voting 50–48 against the debate.

On November 2, eleven more states voted as Louisiana had, banning same-sex marriage via amendments to their state constitutions, with margins approaching the unbelievable in American politics. Many commentators have argued that the prevalence of the issue in fact provided George W. Bush with a crucial margin of support in his re-election.

One such state ban, Nebraska's, was declared unconstitutional by a federal district court in Nebraska on April 25, 2005. Litigation on the issue is under way across the United States, and of course Massachusetts continues to marry same-sex couples who have moved throughout the United States, setting off additional litigation under the argument that the United States Constitution's "full faith and credit" clause, as well as the Fourteenth Amendment's guarantees of equal protection and due process, require recognition of their marriages as all other out-of-state marriages are routinely recognized throughout the country.

As we enter the election season, it is impossible to predict the timing of new developments in the legal battles over same-sex marriage, DOMA, the state constitutional amendments, the proposed federal amendment, or the variety of positions that high-profile politicians of both parties might take. But this much is clear: nearly all of the support for same-sex marriage is on the left, nearly all the opposition is on the right. It is not just a "wedge issue." Same-sex marriage is a cleaver issue, for two reasons.

The first argument concerns the morality of same-sex relationships, and the outlines of that argument are so familiar as to bore. Either one believes sex outside of marriage between a man and a woman is sinful and wrong, or one doesn't. There is very little a book of this sort, or any book for that matter, can say to change many opinions on the subject, and I have no intention of trying.

But the second debate around same-sex marriage is a very crucial issue that needs to be argued out in public, in the most civil of conditions, no matter what the left says about the motives of the center-right.

Not once, in all the years since the United States Constitution was ratified in 1789, has any state legislature passed and governor signed a single law opening the institution of marriage to two individuals of the same sex.

Not once.

The federal government has not only not passed such a statute, it adopted the opposite: DOMA.

Every time people have voted on an initiative on the subject, the idea of marriage as being exclusively as between a man and a woman is the winner by huge margins.

In short, every democratic—with a small *d*—exercise on the subject of marriage has validated, confirmed, made obvious and undeniable the position of the people of the United States: marriage is between one man and one woman.

The refusal of the left to accept this proposition and this overwhelming mountain of evidence confirms the essentially undemocratic nature of the left: those on the left do not believe in the equality of voters and the institutions of representative government. They believe in what they believe in.

And that should be repeatedly and emphatically explained on every platform and on every occasion that the issue surfaces.

Same-sex marriage opponents try mightily to avoid this record of popular will expressed through elected representatives or direct initiatives. Via the crude sophistry of vague arguments about segregation and women's rights, they attempt to mount the argument that courts have always had to act to break through repressive majorities suppressing minority rights. Because courts have indeed had to lead on desegregation and in striking down a variety of statutes and regulations disfavoring women, proponents of same-sex marriage celebrate the Massachusetts Supreme Judicial Council as the heir of the Supreme Court's unanimous decision in *Brown v. Board of Education* that "separate" was indeed "not equal."

Of course, the Constitution was amended to remove the stain of slavery, and the Constitution was amended to provide women with the vote. When the Supreme Court acted in both arenas, it did so with a historical judgment already rendered: there were to be no second-class citizens in the United States. A Constitution that had been flawed at its start was corrected, and the Court was fulfilling long-delayed promises when it led on the issue of civil rights.

There is no such predicate on the subject of same-sex marriage. In fact there is the opposite. Courts are imposing their will, not heeding the will of majorities. And that is the crucial issue in 2006 and 2008:

How are we going to govern ourselves? Through the majority vote of nine unelected judges, as Justice Scalia has so memorably put it, or through duly elected representatives and initiatives?

The Democratic left says the former.

Every Republican candidate should return again and again to this subject, and refuse to participate in a shouting match about sexual ethics.

There is hardly an American who does not denounce the absurd, hate-filled speech of extreme anti-homosexual groups who use every opportunity to spew their vile calls for criminalization of sexuality or second-class citizenship for gays and lesbians.

But the debate is not about those nutters, any more than a debate about gun control is a debate over the Columbine killers. The Republican Party must demand of Democrats, and the public must demand of the MSM's questioners of Democratic candidates, one thing: candor on this issue.

The key question is not whether candidate A or B "supports gay marriage." Here's the key question: if DOMA is declared unconstitutional by the Supreme Court, will you support a constitutional amendment preserving either a state option or the definition of marriage as between one man and one woman?

Here's an even simpler version of that: did the Massachusetts Supreme Court decide the same-sex marriage case correctly?

Or another: If your state's highest court mandated same-sex marriage, would you be upset? If so, why? If not, why not?

The MSM has given a pass to the entire Democratic Party on this issue, and for an obvious reason. An overwhelming majority of gays and lesbians would like to be able to marry if they so chose. Given that the MSM is overwhelmingly made up of individuals from elite groups, they are aware of this sentiment, and most likely have close friends and/or family who are gay or lesbian. I do. In fact, everyone, and I think it really is literally "everyone" I count as a friend or colleague, has gay or lesbian friends and/or relatives. No one likes to be thought a bigot, and to discuss this issue on any basis, even this basis of the nature of who governs, is to invite that label, no matter who wrongfully or self-evidently foolish its application.

But is simply easier to avoid the subject, so most candidates and nearly all in the MSM do.

Yet that is a huge failure. What happened with abortion simply cannot be allowed to happen with same-sex marriage: the opening of a deep and endless bitter political divide because courts would not honor their equal branches and rushed to attempt, foolishly and ineffectively, to end a debate prematurely.

Such debates cannot be ended. They must go on and on until a resolution is achieved, and no resolution is permanent, only legitimate. The resolutions imposed by courts are neither.

In his magnificent dissent in the case of *Planned Parenthood v. Casey*, Justice Scalia, who had hoped to see *Roe v. Wade* fully reversed and not merely restructured from incoherent, unconstitutional, and undemocratic to merely unconstitutional and undemocratic, wrote eloquently on the danger of judicial power at flood, when it breaks out of its banks of self-imposed prudence.

Scalia's somber reflections need to be internalized by the GOP and explained to the electorates. The country cannot flourish under the rule of robed elites. We are not far down that road, but far enough to worry any prudent constitutionalist.

This is, in many ways, the GOP's "Sister Souljah moment." The online encyclopedia Wikipedia explains this term (as of September 1, 2005; Wikipedia, being interactive, continually evolves):

In United States politics, a Sister Souljah moment is a politician's public repudiation of an allegedly extremist person, statement, or position perceived to have some association with the politician. Whether sincere or not, such an act of repudiation can appeal to centrist voters, at the cost of alienating some of the politician's allies.

The term originates in the 1992 presidential candidacy of Bill Clinton. In an interview conducted May 13, 1992, the rapper Sister Souljah was quoted in the *Washington Post* as saying: "If black people kill black people every day, why not have a week and kill white people?"

The remark was part of a longer response to the 1992 Los Angeles riots. The quote was later reproduced without its context and widely criticized in the media.

In June 1992, Clinton responded to the quote, saying: "If you took the words 'white' and 'black' and you reversed them, you might think David Duke was giving that speech." Clinton thereby repudiated the "extremist" position that Souljah's quote represented.

Clinton's response was criticized by members and leaders of the Democratic Party's African-American base, such as Jesse Jackson. However, it also produced the image, in the eyes of "moderate" and "independent" voters—particularly white voters—of a centrist politician who was "tough on crime" and "not influenced by special interests." Since moderates and independents represent swing votes, whereas the party base will not usually leave for the other party, Clinton's condemnation probably won him more votes than he lost.

Clinton's Sister Souljah moment, whether born of political calculation or not, was consonant with his larger strategy to move the Democratic Party to a more centrist stance on many issues. Other elements of this centrist strategy included an embrace of Third Way economic policy and close relations with the Democratic Leadership Council. Clinton went on to win the presidency, and the term "Sister Souljah moment" subsequently entered the political lexicon.

The political genius of Bill Clinton recognized that the philosophical center of America, and indeed most of the conservative end of the political spectrum, was deeply committed to civil rights and the idea of equality. At the same time, Clinton understood that most of the center of America and a good portion of the conservative end of the spectrum was suspicious of excessive deference to morally compromised "civil rights leaders" like Jesse Jackson and Al Sharpton, who embodied what the center-right considered to be unjust demands, whether for race-based benefits like medical school admissions or reparations. Clinton shrewdly selected the issue of offensive music and lyrics and a setting that seemed high-risk to rebuke an extreme that no one could defend: a song suggesting that the killing of police was a good thing.

The political center of America is libertarian on matters of sexual practice, and a good portion of the conservative spectrum genuinely "loves the sinner and hates the sin," and despises the hatred of bigots far, far more than the failings of the flesh. A number of the conservatives, perhaps even a majority, would accept any legislative recognition of gay marriage as legitimate though badly decided.

GOP candidates and especially Senate nominees need to find opportunities to communicate this very specific message, and to do so again and again. George W. Bush is the model, never speaking on the issue of marriage without first recognizing that millions of Americans are gay or lesbian and that they all have feelings and families and deserve the respect we should extend to every citizen of the Republic.

Courts that wish to wrongfully and undemocratically impose their policy preferences on America should not be allowed to dictate either

the laws of the United States or the reputations of those who participate in the debates about those laws. As the elections of 2006 loom,
Republican candidates should willingly enter the debate about marriage and the courts, but only with the attitude and rhetoric that
contributes to victories, not the sort that blunders into defeats.

CHAPTER SEVEN

GOP MESSAGE 5

The Democratic Left Is Addicted to Venom, and That Venom Is Poisoning the Political Process

So what hath the blogosphere wrought? The left blogosphere has moved the Democrats off to the left, and the right blogosphere has undermined the credibility of the Republicans' adversaries in Old Media. Both changes help Bush and the Republicans.

—**Michael Barone**, *U.S. News & World Report*, February 5, 2005

I first wrote a version of this chapter for my blog in July 2005, and then delivered a revised version to a conference on the rise of new media held at Hillsdale College in mid-November. Since its drafting and revision, the blogosphere and its amazing synergy with talk radio have continued to shape, indeed transform, politics in America and across the globe.

The implications for American politics are still unclear, but all of them flow from the fact that there are no information hierarchies left. No one—not the president, not Karl Rove, not Howard Dean or Harry Reid or all the network execs acting alone or in concert—no one dictates the news cycle anymore, and no false proposition can survive the attention of the many.

This is great news for the Republican Party for, while it can and often is wrong on many things, it is not wrong on the Global War on Terror, the proper role of judges, or the best policies to further economic growth. Thus the arrival of new media is a boon to the GOP never before seen in modern politics.

At the same time, the Internet has proven to be a horrible factor within the Democratic Party. It's not that the party doesn't understand it—they do, at times even better than the Republicans—but that the Internet has allowed the far-left elements of the Democratic constituency to express their deepest sentiments for all the world to see.

Without the power of sites like Daily Kos, the Democratic Party could be moving much closer to the center-right values of America. But the fund-raising capability and loud megaphone of these Internet liberals, most of whom are so extreme that they have never run a winning campaign or participated in a successful political venture, have compromised much of the Democratic leadership. On this site alone, blog posts have been written by Barack Obama, John Kerry, Ted Kennedy, Barbara Boxer, Jim McDermott, and John Edwards, and they've appeared alongside entries from members alleging the worst kind of poisonous Michael Moore conspiracy theories, including that President Bush has a secret partnership with Osama bin Laden.

The blogosphere can expose the Democratic left for what it truly is, in all its conspiracy-loving anti-American glory. Yet, if understood rightly, it can also offer a decisive and enduring advantage for the GOP.

The Effects of Plumbing on Water Quality

Dean Barnett blogs at Soxblog and writes for the *Weekly Standard*. He is a keen observer of trends in the blogosphere, and beginning with a July 15, 2005, online piece for the *Standard*, charted the lurch toward vulgarity and venom on the left side of the blogosphere. My only quarrel with Barnett's writings on the subject is that he does not fully convey the sea change in politics that has occurred because of the blogs.

Barnett correctly noted in his July piece that blog readers are information junkies and news addicts. Across the political spectrum, blog writers and readers just love the inside game. No matter what the subject, within the blogs there will be deep mines of information that simply never makes it into the MSM because of space considerations that don't exist for bloggers. When a blogger obsesses on a subject, the information just keeps coming and coming.

The blogosphere is a vast set of information pipes, like water pipes, providing the stuff information/news junkies find essential. The old plumbing is still out there—newspapers, television, radio—but blogs have dramatically increased the volume of the information flow.

What Barnett began to outline last year is that the left side of the blogosphere's pipes have a problem. They are made of lead. They are, in fact, poisoning the information they are distributing, and the consequence is the slow poisoning of the Democratic Party.

Barnett correctly notes that the tone on the left side of the blogosphere would repel most Americans who still like even the hottest political arguments delivered within certain rhetorical guidelines. The lefty blogs are training an entire generation of activists to conduct themselves outside those rules, to develop habits that are not only handicaps to persuasion, but are actually almost insurmountable barriers to a huge portion of the independent vote and even a large slice of Democrats. The day after Barnett's piece appeared, one of the left's superstars, Atrios, quoted Horace Mann[1] on the likely outcome of the lessons the lefty blog leaders are teaching their troops: "Habit is a cable; we weave a thread of it each day, and at last we cannot break it."

Mann is correct, of course, and the habits of communication among the lefty blogs are poisonous ones for the Democratic Party.

My friend Sam, an elder and giant of my church, is a rock-ribbed FDR Democrat with whom I have been talking politics for years without making any inroads. I plan to introduce him to the Kos kids so that he can see what his party is becoming. Even if Sam shrugs it off, I know that across the country young left-wing activists are not learning author Saul Alinsky's methods for building coalition, laid out in detail in his work *Rules for Radicals*, on which two generations of liberal activists were raised. They're learning exactly the opposite lessons—call them Kos' rules for marginalizing a message.

But that isn't the most important impact of the lefty blogs. Rather, these blogs are pumping out bad information and flawed analysis. Imagine a faculty of a medical school that consistently and for a period of years taught its students incorrect methods of diagnosis. The damage done would not be limited to the doctors whose education was flawed. The far greater evil would be visited on the patients on the receiving end of the lousy training. Thus are the leading lefty bloggers injuring the lefties and especially the centrist Democrats who read and believe them.

This terrible toll on the reasonability of the center-left is illustrated by an example drawn from the reflexive dismissal by the left of all evidence and argument about a Saddam-al Qaeda connection.

On the same weekend that Atrios was quoting Mann and Barnett's piece was being chewed over by his critics, Washington Monthly's lefty blogger Kevin Drum ran a post[2] that perfectly illustrated the effect of lousy analysis combined with invective combined with the assertion of a conclusion that will harden a position untenable with the public, as has been proven by two cycles of elections.

First, Kevin—who is a pleasant fellow in person, and in my two or three conversations with him has never adopted the tone he routinely embraces on his blog—began by using hyperbole to highlight a post by Glenn Reynold of a link to old, but previously not widely circulated video from ABC News, video that reported on the Clinton-era belief that Saddam was connected with al Qaeda:

> Today's big news in the conservosphere is a six-year old ABC News segment that's been heroically rescued from the "memory hole" and is now being trumpeted as proof—proof dammit!—that Saddam Hussein and Osama bin Laden used to be best buddies and Democrats have known it all along. It's only when George Bush became president that we started denying it.

The tape in question was in fact very interesting, even though it did not contain any new information for people who had studied the connection between al Qaeda and Iraq. The tape was significant for what it told us about media bias against the Saddam-al Qaeda connection story in 2005, not for what it told us about the actual connection. Here's Drum's summary of the video:

> And indeed, the ABC segment reports that Osama's people and Saddam's people had contacts in 1994 in Sudan and in late 1998 in Afghanistan. There's only one problem: this is nothing

new. Nor was it new a year ago, the last time that Instapundit "discovered" this.[3]

I think many fair observers who did not listen to the ABC tape or did not check the Instapundit link Drum referred to would have concluded that Instapundit had reported on the existence of the ABC tape a year ago and that Glenn was recycling news of the video, which was not the case. The video had not previously been reported on by Reynolds or widely known to exist.

Drum, either intentionally or because of sloppy writing, then suggested that the ABC tape was evidence of "conservative amnesia," and that "nothing new" has been reported that weekend. But the surfacing of the ABC segment was news because it was supporting evidence for the fact that the MSM had previously reported allegations of close contacts at the highest levels between Saddam's regime and bin Laden. This reporting had been overlooked in the MSM's repeated barrages of skepticism aimed at any argument that a connection existed. And not only was this a very, very useful bit of tape when it comes time to analyze ABC's uneven coverage of the war, but also having an audio and a video file demonstrating such a thing is a tremendously useful bit of evidence of media bias as audio and video communicate the key facts in a way that the written word does not.

Drum's post that July morning, then, was a widely read blog of the left sloppily reporting a development of interest on the MSM's coverage of a crucial story. This sloppy reporting came at the end of a week when both *Weekly Standard* writer Stephen Hayes[4] and journalist-in-residence at the Foundation for the Defense of Democracies and OpinionJournal.com columnist Claudia Rosett[5] had written crucial updates on the underlying subject of the ABC report. Drum misrepresented an interesting post and ignored the other stories because he—and most lefty bloggers—are so invested in their own narratives of the Saddam-al Qaeda "connection" that they cannot allow contrary evidence to enter their world.

But the example is even more telling. Drum then went on to discuss the central objective of his post: to reassure readers that "[b]oth Saddam and Osama hated the United States. They had a couple of tentative conversations *that never led anywhere. The last ones were in late 1998 or early 1999,* and by the time the war started, the fundamentalist Sunnis of al-Qaeda and the secular Baathists of Iraq hadn't so much as exchanged notes for four years." (emphasis added)

As evidence for this proposition, Drum cited the 9-11 Commission report, which concluded "[b]ut to date we have seen no evidence that these or the earlier contacts ever developed into a collaborative operational relationship." My readers can judge for themselves whether Drum's readers might have been better served by more extensive quoting from page sixty-six of the 9-11 Commission report, or pointers to subsequent analysis like that done by Hayes and Rosett, but surely those readers cannot be well served when Drum transformed the 9-11 Commission's conclusion of "to date we have seen no evidence" of a "collaborative operational relationship" into conclusions that there was nothing to the idea of a connection and no more thinking to be done on the issue or evidence to be reviewed. Drum was trying, ineffectively and rather desperately, to close the case on the connection, because the connection makes an airtight case for the invasion of Iraq. Preempting the development of new evidence, or a re-examination of shared assumptions as demonstrated by the ABC tape, is a goal of the left side of the blogosphere, though one it has never been able to reach. Milblogger Major K, blogging from Iraq the same week as Drum's post, showed why.[6]

> The press is all over the idea that by fighting terrorists, we have offended them so badly that they attack us. WHAT!?!

Zarqawi was here before we were. There is an old terrorist training camp about 20 miles south of my location right now. It is no longer functioning because we are here. It was bustling with activity when Saddam was in charge. Most of the guys that we hunt are the al Qaeda affiliates—the same kind of scum that hit New York and now London.

I doubt very much if Drum wrote to inform Major K that he was sadly mistaken. Zarqawi is the inconvenient and impossible to dismiss link between Saddam and al Qaeda, an Afghanistan-trained and Baghdad-located al Qaeda terrorist.

I am not trying here to review the debate over "the connection," but rather to note that Drum's post on July 16, 2005, was an example that in the lead pipes of the blogosphere, there is no open debate on matters of the canon, no room for new information, or even the remote possibility that on any issue related to the al Qaeda-Saddam connection, the left could be wrong.

Sir Thomas Gresham's "law" that "bad money drives out good" applies to information and analysis[7] as well as currency, and that law is at work every day on the left side of the blogosphere, where lousy logic and terrible habits of mind are being nurtured and praised. Saddam could testify at his trial that he and Osama had been in secret communication and coordinated operational alliance since 1996 and Drum and allies would still find a way to dismiss the testimony. The effect of such deep close-mindedness is to seal off the left from the mainstream, and to alert the American electorate that the forces behind the Democratic Party will not govern in response to facts, but in response to what they want to believe to be facts—a dangerous and self-destructive refusal to see the world as it is.

Copper Pipes and the Water Supply

. . . .

This analysis of the center-right blogosphere's impact on politics is concerned primarily with the impact of the largest center-right bloggers, taken from N.Z. Bear's ecosystem traffic rankings,[8] though there are exceptions to some of these general observations

First, I believe the methods of argument among the center-right blogs are much, much more fact-specific, and much less prone to vulgarity, profanity, or the sort of personal attacks that create barriers to new readership than the largest blogs on the left. No matter what you think of Betsy Newmark's Betsy's Page[9]—Newmark is an AP history teacher who has a devoted following—her language and overall approach will never be in itself an obstacle to a reader's return to her blog. Keeping this culture of presentation and argument matters a great deal to the future growth of the center-right blogosphere and certainly the influence of the center-right bloggers. At the group blog where I am now executive editor, BeyondTheNews.com's collaboration of talk-show hosts Bill Bennett, Dennis Prager, Michael Medved, and others, there are standards that never have to be articulated because each of the posters brings a deportment that doesn't allow him to degenerate into the self-defeating tactics on the left.

The early major bloggers of the center-right were much more likely to be lawyers, law professors, journalists, or authors than those on the left. This set a tone and a style that has been very useful to new bloggers, who I think clearly adopted some of the approaches developed by Instapundit[10] and Powerline[11], for example. The ranks of leading center-right bloggers continue to grow, and recent arrivals of pros like Michelle Malkin[12], Jonathan Last[13], and Human Events Online[14] have brought enormous energy and professional skill to the center-right. NationalReview.com[15] is dedicated to finding new blog talent and launching those writers with great fanfare and support.

Another legion of professional communicators—pastors, scholars, and professors like Al Mohler[16] and John Mark Reynolds[17]—have also enriched the center-right blogosphere in recent years, widening a path cleared by such Godbloggers as MarkDRoberts.com and demonstrating how the Christian communicator can expand his or her areas of commentary beyond theology to politics and culture.

The center-right blogosphere is simply more professional about its reporting and more vigorous in its investigations. Ed Morrissey,[18] for example, finds a story like the Gomery Inquiry testimony that involved Canadian corruption, and immediately moved to ignore that country's ban on publishing information on the case, instead pursuing it relentlessly, with support from center-right bloggers eager to call attention not to themselves but Morrissey. That example combined the specialization and accreditation functions prevalent on the right, and every time a blog-driven story appears and the specialization and accreditation cycles repeat, it makes the overall center-right blogosphere stronger. And it does happen again and again. Unlike the MSM which grew up on a culture of "scoop" and "exclusive," and loathed to credit its competition with breakthroughs, the center-right is a vast co-op of sorts, wedded to the idea that everyone wins by linking and attribution.

ConfirmThem[19] and RedState[20] became must-reads for every SCOTUS reporter who took his or her job seriously during the showdown over the "constitutional option," and then the Roberts and Alito nominations, in part because the already existing big blogs on the center-right welcomed both efforts. PoliPundit[21], Daly Thoughts[22], and Patrick Ruffini[23] are tremendously influential among the Beltway types who obsess over politics because they are reliable editors of the avalanche of political news that hits the media every day. (Ruffini has now gone inside the RNC, where he is revolutionizing its news dissemination operation.) What used to be a cottage industry on the marketing of "inside" political news that The Hotline and ABC's The

Note dominated is now free of charge to all comers, no longer hopelessly biased leftward, and is in fact dominated by center-right bloggers who are working all day long and most weekends.

The blogosphere can act with stunning speed. When the scandal surrounding Air America's start-up funding first surfaced at Radioequalizer's Brian Maloney's site, his work was cited and expanded on by Michelle Malkin and others. As I relayed their findings on air, a listener sent me a link to the Gloria Wise Boys and Girls Club IRS Form 990s, and so I posted those for others to work over, and on and on it went. Then Maloney and Malkin combined to stagger more comprehensive reports, and after a few days the MSM was obliged to begin to report the story.

There is also an enormous built-in advantage of having the center-right in power at the time of the rise of the blogosphere. This cannot be underestimated. It helps when, for example, Lynne Cheney remarked on *Hardball* that she read my blog, Instapundit, Powerline and *National Review*'s Jim Geraghty[24] every day. "Hmmm," say the influencers when they hear such a thing. "Perhaps we should be reading what Lynne Cheney is reading."

I am fairly certain that a declaration of blog reading habits by, say, West Virginia's Robert Byrd might not have the same impact.

Beyond simply the attention and information the blogs get from the political majority in power, the fact that the administration has an agenda to be debated and usually supported also infuses the center-right with objectives beyond electoral politics, which made it more responsible than the left has proven to be in the years since the blogs got started in 1999. Trying to help accomplish something as difficult as, say, Social Security reform obliges center-right bloggers to do homework and develop ideas, not merely to push obstruction as a political end. Even when the effort does not initially succeed, the skill sets of evidence assembly and argument don't vanish when Congress adjourns.

Then there are the milblogs, blogs run by active-duty military personnel or veterans, which are quite popular generally and enormously
esteemed by the center-right blogosphere while pretty much ignored
by the lefty blogs. The postings of Mudville,[25] Blackfive,[26] Smash,[27]
FroggyRuminations,[28] Major K, and others are widely linked on the
center-right because of its nearly consistent support for the GWOT
and appreciation of the expertise and sacrifice of the soldiers, sailors,
airmen, and Marines on the front lines. While the active-duty milbloggers remain on the whole apolitical, their belief in their mission,
which is not merely debated on the lefty blogs but often denounced
in the harshest of terms, has made milbloggers in turn generous in
their links to those that support their mission.

Finally, the intellectual seriousness of the center-right blogs is simply light years ahead of that on the left. That seriousness means an
appreciation for argument, self-correction, and a willingness to absorb
and respond to new information, which are habits that if transferred
to center-right activists generally and the GOP specifically will
strengthen effectiveness at every level.

Here's one example from my own blog, which to be fair in terms of
comparative analysis I took from the same week as Kevin Drum's post
described above.

On Thursday of that week I wrote a piece for the WeeklyStan-
dard.com, "Breeding Stupidity"[29] which took aim at "the left's claim
that Iraq is a breeding ground for terrorists," and specifically at the
assertion that the London bombers had been "inflamed by Britain's
participation in the Iraq war." "While it is theoretically possible that
some jihadists were forged as a result of the invasion of Iraq," I wrote,
"no specific instance of such a terrorist has yet been produced."

Two days later, some evidence for the "breeding ground" theory did
in fact surface, in the *Boston Globe's* report of two new studies, one
from Israel and one from Saudi Arabia.[30] Because contrary evidence

should be confronted and analyzed, and judgments modified, if appropriate, I immediately brought them to my blog readers' attention. If the studies are persuasive, the Iraq front in the GWOT has to be re-evaluated based on the number of jihadists it spawns and what happens to them. I did not find them so, especially after interviewing one of the authors on air, but that is not the point. The point is that like most on the center-right in the new media, I am eager to debate all the evidence on any particular fashion and to do so with civility and at length.

Yet my point here is not to conduct that particular debate or even open it, but to instead demonstrate what I think is the widespread habit on the center-right of confronting contrary evidence and tackling it, of reading the other side's best case and responding, rather than taking the leftist tactic of screaming obscenities at the messenger.

In other words, the center-right is a great influence on center-right politics because it is practicing the ultimate skill in a democracy: persuasive argument.

Some final points. The political left benefited for three decades from the very left-wing bias of the MSM. The political right is now benefiting from the still overwhelming left-wing bias of the MSM because the center-right blogs almost daily expose that bias, and the cumulative effect of those exposures is the rapid fall in MSM credibility. I think this has been accompanied by a tumble in the credibility of those whom the MSM endorses. "The MSM is on your side?" a good slice of the electorate thinks to itself. "Then you must be from the left, and we probably aren't getting the whole story." The delegitimization of MSM has helped delegitimize the left as well, though Michael Moore and Howard Dean get the most credit for that.

Next, and I say this objectively, as a group the center-right bloggers are funnier (e.g. FratersLibertas[31], Scott Ott's Scrappleface[32]) and far more skilled with words than their lefty counterparts (*Minneapolis*

Star-Tribune columnist and author/blogger Lileks[33] versus, well, any-one.) We have cartoonist Chris Muir[34], the funniest three-panel political cartoonist at work today. They have to pretend to like Ted Rall.[35]

Talent matters. A lot. And Mark Steyn hasn't even started yet.

These are copper pipes providing good, clean information with great pressure behind it. It is a great, great advantage, and not one that can be overcome for years and years because of the market share achieved by the dominant lefty blogs.

If Kos and Atrios really cared about their announced political goals, they'd shutter their doors or conduct an extensive reformation of their blogging habits. There's not a chance in the world of their following, much less even considering, such advice, which is why I am so will-ing to give it.

But these advantages are not necessarily permanent, though the deep bitterness on the left side of the web will be difficult to purge, and the effects of Michael Moore and the Daily Kos may endure for decades, crippling not just this but the next generation of liberal-left activists. The best guarantee of continued center-right domination of the new platform is continued insistence by the collective of high standards in terms of style and objectivity and immediate self-correc-tion of error.

The good news is that these red state qualities show no signs of eroding. And in the long term, no amount of lefty poison will win the day.

CHAPTER EIGHT

THE GOP'S NECESSARY DISCIPLINE

Smile When You Say That, Mister

The soul in which philosophy dwells should by its health make even the body healthy. It should make its tranquility and gladness shine out from within; should form in its own mold the outward demeanor, and consequently arm it with a graceful pride, an active and joyous bearing, and a contented and good-natured countenance. The surest sign of wisdom is constant cheerfulness; her state is like that of things above the moon, ever serene.

—**Montaigne**, "On the Education of Children,"
Book I, Essay 26

"The surest sign of wisdom is constant cheerfulness." That is crucial advice for electoral politics in all ages, but especially in the age of terror. Cheerfulness has distinguished great wartime leaders, even when it is mixed with deep resolve or even apparent sadness.

Lincoln, Churchill, FDR, Ronald Reagan—all four of these men understood that the ability to communicate confidence through good cheer and gentle, though occasionally sharp-edged, humor were crucial ingredients in the mix of leadership traits that marked them as great leaders.

George W. Bush understands this as well, and his cheerfulness is a great strength in the various confrontations he has had with his political opponents. That cheerfulness has not been unbroken, of course, but it is a defining mark of his presidency, and a crucial lesson for GOP leadership and supporters in the coming campaigns of 2006 and 2008.

Perhaps the best way of understanding the value of good cheer as a conveyor of confidence and competence is to examine the effects of the opposite attitude. The rhetoric of the left is the best place to find the near total absence of good cheer, and to study the effects of that absence.

Dean Barnett, the writer and blogger I referred to in Chapter Seven, has contributed articles on the evolution of the blogosphere and political activism to the *Weekly Standard* and his posts on his blog Soxblog are crucial essays on what is happening on the left. On August 16, 2005, Barnett posted a profound essay on demeanor, titling it "Advice to an Angry Young Blogger." In his piece, Barnett talked about how his article about a liberal blogger named Bob Brigham was greeted by an obscenity-laced response when it included a minor mistake. I reprint an excerpt here with permission:

I know [Brigham's] response was just a manifestation of the angry young blogger shtick, but it's tired. All the obscenities, all the rage—what do Brigham and his ilk think they accomplish? Do they not see how pathetic such antics make them look?

Left wing bloggers like Brigham are often guilty of confusing and conflating "straight talk" with vulgar talk. Look, I'm no prude, especially when it comes to coarse language. Those who personally know me, and especially those who have played golf with me, view me as a uniquely unlikely champion for obscenity-free communication.

But politics is different from one's rec-room or the golf course. There are a bunch of people who find obscenities offensive. In politics (and bloggers like Brigham are in politics), there is no need to gratuitously offend a segment of the voting society with coarse language. And yet Brigham and many of his cohorts insist on writing like they're politically obsessed Quentin Tarantino characters.

I started this essay by talking about shoring up one's perceived weaknesses. For left wing bloggers, the doubts they have to overcome is whether they are mature enough and sophisticated enough to take their act public. Some of them seem to know this. Chris Bowers at MyDD is doubtlessly one of the brightest liberal bloggers around, and he eschews a constant stream of obscenities in favor of well thought through and maturely expressed postings. Bowers is also seeking office, and he's smart enough to understand all of this. The bigger question is, why aren't all of them?

What Barnett is sincerely trying to communicate to Brigham is that there is no upside at all in politics for profanity, and especially for those who use vulgarity and profanity to try and score points. While there is always a market for such writing or speech, it is a very limited market indeed, nowhere near the majority of the electorate needed to win elections and assemble coalitions. The resort to profanity and vulgarity in order to communicate anger or even passion inevitably drives away a large part of the audience that wants no part of the crudity.

The proof of this observation is in the public speech of everyone in Congress, and indeed in all of the elected offices of the United States. Elected officials simply do not use the sort of language Brigham used in his writing or his missive to Barnett. The world of youth culture in which vulgarity and profanity proliferate is completely separate from the world of politics and governance, no matter what inhabitants of the former may tell themselves.

The reason is simple: governance requires a clear head and a control of one's own passions. The inability to control one's passions is a sign of instability and is very dangerous in a political leader. Passion can fuel political movements and even revolutions, but usually not popular ones. And once in power the passionate and undisciplined ruler creates havoc and leaves devastation in his wake.

Vulgar and crude speech, then, is a sign of an untrustworthy leader, and possibly of a fanatic. Temperate speech, and especially good humor and cheerfulness, are indications of exactly the opposite: They signify a composed soul and a good character that is unlikely to be captured by excessive passion and wild causes.

This admonition to cheerfulness in demeanor and speech has many practical applications. Here are a few:

- Self-effacement is the most prized of all attributes among candidates
- Never be in a hurry to demean your opponent's character
- Always find something to praise in your opponent's record and life
- Never, ever, attack an opponent's family

- Be quick to rebuke friends and allies who go overboard in attacking opponents
- Try to find something to appropriate from your opponent's proposals and records, praising it as his or hers, but modifying it to demonstrate how it is flawed in the original
- Almost always speak well of the media even when it is attacking you, but turn on it with passion if it attacks your family or close friends
- Learn to tell a joke. If you lack the timing to tell jokes, then lampoon your own limited ability at joke telling.
- And, most crucial of all, always be smiling. Always. The camera is never off, and there is no private sphere for a candidate running for high office. Training in cheerfulness eventually produces the real thing.

In the campaign of 2004, it was John Kerry's demeanor more than anything else that drove away voters. Whether it was the low-voiced paranoia he whispered to a union supporter along a receiving line when he thought the microphones were off: "These guys, they are the #$@^% ever" or the callous attempt to make the vice president's daughter an issue in the debates, time and again Kerry could not conceal his contempt for his opponents or his willingness to go below the belt if he thought that would win. Rather than confront the charges of the Swift Boat veterans head on, especially their charge, proven beyond any doubt, that Kerry had not been in Cambodia on an illegal mission on Christmas eve 1968, which he had repeatedly and emphatically put forward even on the floor of the Senate, Kerry and his surrogates attacked and attacked the vets. Every time Kerry lashed out, and every time his surrogates slashed at the highly decorated vets, Kerry's stock fell.

Simply put, the American people are not quick to embrace sour and gloomy leadership. They like the Ronald Reagan/George H. W. Bush/Bill Clinton/George W. Bush approach to politics.

The old media and the new media on the center-right play by the old rules of decency and propriety, though there are a few exceptions. By contrast, the new media of the left is drenched in the extreme speech and charges that most Americans find unsettling evidence of fanaticism.

The habits that are being formed on the left will adversely affect a generation of Democratic candidates and causes, and may succeed in marginalizing the Democratic Party beyond even its already weakened state.

Because of the vitriol on the left, the temptation exists to respond in kind. That would be a huge mistake. Keep in mind that the country, though favoring the GOP presently—Michael Barone suspects that it is a 51–48 red/blue split right now, a significant shift from the 49–49 country of 2000—is still closely divided. The left is busy offending a crucial percentage of the electorate, and the center-right should not do anything to obstruct this self-destruction.

Thus every candidate and operative ought to follow closely the lead of the president and vice president, of party chair Ken Mehlman and congressional leadership: angry words ought to be reserved for our mortal enemies abroad, not for political opponents at home.

CHAPTER NINE

THE POTENTIAL DISASTER OF CIVIL WAR WITHIN THE GOP

Border Security

In early 2005, I had the opportunity, rare and much appreciated, to talk with a "senior administration official," perhaps even one who had been to an "undisclosed location" a time or two, on what I viewed as the biggest threat to a generation of Republican majorities.

I don't recall the exact wording, but I did ask this official to consider not just the human cost but also the governing consequences of a significant terrorist attack on American soil conducted by terrorists who had entered the country illegally through the U.S.–Mexican border.

Had Atta and his gang entered in that fashion, we would now be well advanced on the project of building a wall and a highway to patrol it along the U.S.–Mexican border. Eventually a terrorist will cross that border and do that deed. Eventually a wall will be built. There is no advantage in postponing the inevitable in this instance. The GOP needs to get moving.

There is a deep nativist streak in the United States, but it is narrow. I am typing the first draft of this chapter as I cross the Atlantic in an airplane. James Hewitt crossed in a ship in 1868, from Ulster (its suburb of Saintfield, to be exact) first to New York, then to western Pennsylvania to work in the coal mines there, and then to a farm in Saybrook township, Ohio. One of his sons, my grandfather, got lucky with a small inheritance and in his thirties went on to law school and to become an Ashtabula judge, his grandson a veteran of World War II and a lawyer much admired in Ohio, with a great-grandson so thoroughly American that I don't hesitate to dispense advice every day on how the country should be led—all in the space of less than 140 years, a blink of the historical eye.

Given this personal history and a similar story on my mother's German–Green Irish side of the family, it should come as no surprise that I think the nativist impulse is ignorant and can be ignored.

Yet the demand for security is not nativist, and is in fact the first call on the Constitution's promises, and cannot be set aside.

Some demagogues have not figured this out, talk-radio hosts among them. They confuse the demand for border security with the demand for "culture" and "language."

The GOP needs to be first on security so it can hold the line on citizenship and one nation for all who come here. But it also must firmly and repeatedly reject nativist impulses in all of their many forms.

President Bush understands the need to welcome, and surely no one can argue that he is not every day and every way committed to fighting the GWOT. But the visible expression of that need is a wall. Every GOP candidate should be calling for it, and the GOP Congress should be demanding its beginning.

At the same time, every GOP candidate has to guard against the nativist impulse. The movie *Gangs of New York* was not much admired by critics, but I thought Daniel Day-Lewis did a fine job of conveying the panic felt by the economically stressed at the arrival of large numbers of perceived competitors. It's foolish, wrong, and short-sighted.

That panic remains in 2006 in many precincts of America, though for Californians like me it should be hard to believe when we drive past the strawberry and lettuce fields in which the farm laborer toils. California and now Texas are "majority minority" states, and the Latino population that will guide those states' futures need to be embraced and honored, and not in any way repelled.

The good news is that they are overwhelmingly Catholic and deeply so, with an unshakeable faith in the Church. The bad news is that some GOP politicians cannot resist the cheap fix that helps their poll numbers while injuring the party as a whole.

Former governor Pete Wilson is responsible for me meeting my wife and I genuinely admire his intelligence and skill, and especially his love for the Golden State. But Proposition 187 was his Watergate. What a disaster to appeal to the voters of California on the issue of illegal immigration! May it never be repeated.

If children have been brought to the United States illegally, they should be educated and immunized and cared for as we would any child. If an employer hires an illegal, he should be fined. If the illegal is a law-abiding and employed man or woman, we should seek to regularize his or her status and offer security, though not citizenship, and perhaps tax him or her at a higher rate as punishment for indifference to our borders.

But we need to lock down those borders, and do it yesterday. So what did the "senior administration official" say? "Study the president's comments closely." For the sake of the future of the party, I agree.

CHAPTER TEN

LOOKING AHEAD 1

Hillary/Obama and the Last Gasp of the Democratic Party

Sixty-four percent of Americans over the age of eighteen voted in the presidential election of 2004. A very high percentage of those registered to vote actually did so; 89 percent or 126 million Americans voted, according to the Census Bureau.[1]

According to the Bureau, of the nation's 24,910,000 blacks over the age of 18, only 16,035,000 were registered to vote, and only 14,010,000 actually voted in the election. More than 10 million potential black voters—10,890,000 if we use the Bureau's figures—did not vote.

By comparison, and again according to the Census Bureau, only 7,578,000 of the 16,088,000 Hispanic

American citizens over the age of 18 voted. (Only 9,308,000 are registered to vote.)

Which means more than 8,500,000 eligible Hispanics did not vote.

John Kerry lost the popular vote to George W. Bush by 3,012,497 votes.

Study these numbers carefully. They represent the last chance for the Democrats to reclaim the White House in the foreseeable future.

I think the nomination of Hillary Clinton as the Democrats' standard-bearer in 2008 is inevitable absent an unexpected event. Senator Clinton appears to be gearing up for the run, and if she wants the nomination, it is hers. Former Virginia governor Mark Warner, New Mexico governor Bill Richardson, failed nominee John Kerry, balloon about-to-burst Howard Dean, plain as vanilla Evan Bayh—in truth, they are all running for veep.

And when former President Clinton introduces his wife on the closing night of the Democratic Convention in Cleveland the frenzy among Democrats and the MSM will reach an almost unimaginable level.

As will the fear among Republicans.

And when Hillary gives a great, great speech penned by Sidney Blumenthal, the frenzy and the fear will both mount higher.

And when running mate Barack Obama and his wife, Michelle, join the Clintons on stage, and then Chelsea and nine-year-old Malia and six-year-old Natasha join their parents, well, the power surge felt by the Democrats and their elite media pals might just short out the MSM circuits.

Whoever the nominee of the GOP will be, he will be down by fifteen points on the night the Democratic convention closes. When the Republican convention opens a few weeks later in Minneapolis the task of the nominee will be to speak directly to the American people not about Senators Clinton and Obama, but about the Democratic

Party as a whole and its inability to keep the nation secure in this perilous time of war.

Vice presidential nominee Condoleezza Rice will have set that tone and painted that picture, but it will be the presidential nominee's task to assure the American people that their security depends upon the steady resolve and accumulated experience of the Republican Party's many levels of leadership. He will not be experienced in the burdens of the presidency, of course, but the choice, so obvious, between a return to the blinkered and disastrous security policies of the Clinton nineties or a continuation of the aggressive forward defense of the Bush years will be the choice on which the election depends. The nominee must make that case the night of his nomination and every day thereafter.

Hillary (and Bill) are going to have a huge built-in advantage in the MSM, and the Obama Bonanza will also be a very significant advantage, and not just in the expected impact on African American registration and turnout. Having seen Obama in person at the Democratic National Convention in 2004, I can attest to his presence and his delivery. His youth will be an advantage almost as significant as his race. Concerns over inexperience will quickly be swallowed up by the predictable rejoinder about how this ticket, unique in American history, brings with it prior White House experience like no other ticket ever has, including FDR's 1944 run.

Even if the economy remains strong, gas prices fall, and new media continues to expand in audience and influence, still the Democrats have to be considered favorites to reclaim 1600 Pennsylvania a little over thirty months from now. Not the Senate or the House, but the presidency, yes.

This is why the GOP has to be absolutely cold-hearted in this nomination cycle. In any other year when the stakes were not so high nor the opponents so extraordinarily well positioned, the party that loves to bleed itself on a monthly basis will have to avoid every self-inflicted wound and unite earlier and with more conviction than ever before. And it will have to be behind someone other than an incumbent nominee.

Unless the new Supreme Court moves quickly, the absurd rules of campaign finance brought about by the McCain-Feingold disaster for free speech will still govern 2008, which means that the Democrats' huge money advantage will remain locked in due to the almost maniacal obsession of George Soros and the built-in advantage of paycheck deduction–accorded unions.

Democrats will also benefit from the energy born of desperation, because the underlying realities of realignment are obvious to the Democratic Party pros. They know the new census will send even more electoral power to the red states. They also know that their long-time allies in the old media are losing influence at a burn rate that is startling, and that they have nothing at all like the new media network to replace the old elites and do battle with the powerhouses of talk radio and the web.

They are, in short, staring at collapse on the horizon. They know it. I know it. You must know it as well.

They are going to throw everything they can at this race, and they will be relentless.

If you thought Rathergate was a low point for the MSM in its bias against the GOP, a floor that could not fall any farther, be prepared to dig a cellar.

Parties do die, but never willingly. The Democratic Party is deeply ill, and its disfigurement by the anti-American left is a major problem for a country that needs a healthy two-party system. America needs two parties that, while in agreement on the essential goodness and indeed greatness of the American Republic, go hammer and tong at each other over a host of issues, including tax policy, environmental protection, space exploration, health care delivery, social security, and Medicare reform.

I have long believed that the old guard of the Democratic Party— the Walter Mondales, the George Mitchells, the John Breauxs, the Sam Nunns, the Les Aspins—has watched in horror as the hard left infiltrated and then took control of the party that had been weakened by its Vietnam experience, crippled by Jimmy Carter's languid and ambiguous commitment to FDR and JFK internationalism, and then hollowed out by the "me-first-and-only" presidency of Bill Clinton. The weakened party was unprepared to fight off the left's charge, and when Michael Moore showed up in the presidential box at the party's 2004 Boston convention, there was no one left to eject him or demand Carter do so. The walls had been breached long ago, and not only were there no gatekeepers, there weren't even any gates.

Now these aging warhorses have one last shot, and while the Clintons are still the very embodiment of self-serving ambition, they aren't creatures of the hard left in the way the Gore and Kerry campaigns were at their core. The old Democratic Party elites tell themselves that if they can just get the White House back one more time, they can take back the party as well, purging and rebuilding from a position of strength, credentialing a new generation of center-left activists on domestic policy while rebuffing and retooling the party's tattered reputation on national security and the global war on terror.

If they miss this shot, the purge will be conducted by the other side. "Thorough it will be, and merciless," Yoda might say.

The left was willing to settle for Howard Dean as the party's chair in early 2005, and they will also be willing to sign on to a fusion ticket led by Hillary in 2008 because they believe that, unlike her husband, Hillary really is one of them, just with better manners. They don't doubt her deep contempt for the center-right, or her ability to hold a grudge or put the knife in. She'll do just fine in their view. They know that if she wins back 1600 Pennsylvania Avenue, they will get their share of the spoils.

Hillary brings everyone to the effort, and Senator Obama will energize a base that has never really grasped its leverage on American politics.

The presidential election of 2008 will be the last election in a generation in which the modern Democratic Party will be genuinely competitive if it loses.

Dems know that. Republicans need to know it as well. This is why uniting around a successor to President Bush is so important.

CHAPTER ELEVEN

LOOKING AHEAD 2

The Bush Succession

The last genuine "wide open" hunt for the GOP nomination for president was 1968. Some folks like to point to the 1976 primary battle between Gerald Ford and Ronald Reagan as an "open" fight for the nomination, but a sitting president has huge advantages, and Ford used them all. Some folks like to point to 1980, but all that John Connolly and George H. W. Bush could manage was to force Ronald Reagan to prove he wasn't too old. Once Reagan did that, the nomination was his.

Similarly in 1988, 1996, and 2000, the early frontrunner had reasons to be so declared, and the first President Bush, Senator Dole, and the second President

Bush efficiently secured their nods from their party's loyal base after Pat Buchanan, Lamar Alexander, and John McCain had their fun.

The Republican Party base almost always nominates the most conservative, loyal Republican with the best chance of winning in the fall. Eisenhower in 1952 is the only real exception, and that's the sort of exception that proves this rule: conservative, loyal Republicans nominate conservative, loyal Republicans, and conservative, loyal Republicans dominate the GOP nominating process. Perhaps more than anything else, this attachment to nominees who have been attached to the party's principles and to the party through good times and bad is what has defined the GOP since 1968.

If Vice President Cheney wanted the nomination in 2008, it would be his. Period. Senator McCain might challenge him, but it would again end in tears for the Arizona maverick for the same reason McCain's 2000 campaign folded up: the base thinks he's a great American, a lousy senator, and a terrible Republican—and the base is right.

But Dick Cheney—bold, bright, stand up comic–quick Dick Cheney—now there's the sort of nominee who would sweep the primaries. Really: he's the most conservative, loyal Republican other than W on the national stage.

GOP primary voters fancy themselves, with good reason, as serious responsible people who know a thing or two. They will tell each other and everyone else who will listen that Dick Cheney might not be flashy, might not be a smiling, backslapping Bill Clinton, but that he can be trusted to do the smart and necessary things a president must do in wartime. He's a tough guy, too. And the GOP loves a tough guy who can handle a wise guy like Joe Lieberman or dust down a smooth trial lawyer like John Edwards. Provided he's loyal. And conservative.

Except the vice president isn't running, though I suppose it isn't possible to rule out the sort of change of plans that would be like lightning just prior to New Hampshire, sparing the veep the pain-in-the-neck stomping through fifty state fairgrounds and Lincoln Day/Memorial Day/Fourth of July/Labor Day lunches, dinners, and receptions in remote locations across the country. But that is impossible to predict, whereas the candidacies of McCain, former New York mayor Rudy Giuliani, Senate Majority Leader Bill Frist, Massachusetts governor Mitt Romney, and Virginia senator George Allen are simply givens at this writing.

All five are doing what has to be done to run, and whether one or more drop out before the first farmer makes the first speech at the first Iowa caucus, they are all running as of the spring of 2006 and will be for the next eighteen months. I expect all five to at least make it through the money and talent primaries, wherein each rushes to raise the dollars to be "competitive," and to attract the campaign talent necessary to strategize and implement a winning approach to the nomination.

All are very good men, obviously. Bad men do not get to the heady air of potential presidencies in the modern age. It takes an enormous talent just to get to the starting line. But none of them, not one, meets the dual criteria that have long determined the ultimate nominee.

The three senators all took pratfalls in 2005 of the sort that are not easily recovered from. All three challenged President Bush's conduct of the Global War on Terror, and the base both approves of that conduct and disapproves of disloyalty. Senator McCain was already in deep trouble with the base because of his campaign finance fiasco that unleashed George Soros and for midwifing the reviled "Gang of 14" deal that preserved the filibuster to die another day, but Senators Frist and Allen voted for a Senate resolution on November 15, 2005, that was widely and correctly interpreted as a rebuke of President Bush. The roar of disapproval from the GOP base was instantaneous. Majority Leader Frist was already burdened with a "weak leadership" reputation, so last fall's tumble hurt him more than it did Senator Allen, but both men emerged damaged from their votes on the issue.

There are other new dynamics at work as well: the approach of Hillary and the quite obvious ruthlessness with which the next campaign will be waged.

There's a continued urgency in Republican politics. Most GOP primary voters know that we are in a war for our very lives and continued existence as a country. They know that if one of our Islamist enemies obtains the ability to nuke an American city, they will not hesitate to do so. They also know that the Democratic Party does not grasp this urgent reality.

The GOP primary voters know the stakes, then, and I think are thus uncoupled from their traditional, almost impossible to overcome habits of nominating the most conservative candidate capable of winning. But I don't think they have abandoned the loyalty test, which is why the trio of senators, and maybe a fourth in Nebraska's Chuck Hagel, hurt themselves by appearing to be other than rock-solid supporters of the White House on the GWOT.

There's a good reason for this. Loyalty to party is a good indication of reliability in judgment and predictability in response. The willingness to hang with a party through thick or thin, with its nominees and leadership, communicates judgment, maturity, predictability, and stability.

Senator McCain will never overcome his three strikes on the issue of party loyalty, though of course there is no question that his loyalty to country has been tested and proven far beyond that of any other candidate since Washington.

But McCain is not a "party man." Not remotely so. Three quick reminders:

First, there is his outburst against the base of the party made in Virginia Beach, Virginia, on February 29, 2000, after his loss in the South Carolina primary to President Bush. McCain blamed some religious conservatives for that loss, and although he went out of his way to praise Gary Bauer, James Dobson, and Chuck Colson, he blasted away at a vast group of religious conservatives:

> I am a pro-life, pro-family fiscal conservative and advocate of a strong defense. And yet, Pat Robertson, Jerry Falwell, and a few Washington leaders of the pro-life movement call me an unacceptable presidential candidate. They distort my pro-life positions and smear the reputations of my supporters. Why? Because I don't pander to them. Because I don't [subscribe] to their failed philosophy that money is our message. I believe in the cause of conservative reform... The Republican Party will prevail because of our principles... not special interest money or empire or ego. The union bosses who have subordinated the interests of working families to their own ambitions, to their desire to preserve their own political power at all costs, are mirror images of Pat Robertson.

Even opponents of Pat Robertson and Jerry Falwell within the GOP recoiled at this blunderbuss approach, realizing that for millions of Americans, taking shots at any pastor means taking shots at all pastors. With this ill-tempered outburst, McCain branded himself as unreliable in the eyes of millions of GOP primary voters who, though they might never have given a breath's worth of praise to Robertson, have to conclude that McCain's willingness to purge some GOP loyalists could easily expand.

McCain's second strike was the disastrous McCain-Feingold overhaul of the nation's campaign finance laws, an ill-conceived and poorly written bit of posing that birthed George Soros and MoveOn.Org. McCain has never publicly admitted that his brainchild turned out to be the public policy equivalent of Rosemary's Baby.

The last chance for McCain came after his long effort at rehab during the 2004 campaign. He gamely went to bat for Bush, addressed the GOP convention in the strongest terms, and the memory of his tepid rejection of the Kerry approach in the spring when Kerry tried to woo McCain onto a "fusion" ticket faded. McCain did himself no good when he attempted to dismiss the charges of the Swift Boat vets without a hearing that the public obviously was willing to grant, and, at least with regard to Kerry's preposterous "Christmas Eve in Cambodia in 1968" claim, turned out to exonerate the Swifties.

Yet McCain had positioned himself to be at least a plausible primary candidate. But then came his announcement on *Hardball* that he would oppose the filibuster-ending "constitutional option."

The words were not even out of his mouth when his campaign ended. McCain hadn't warned the leadership. He hadn't told the White House. He hadn't consulted his Arizona colleague Jon Kyl, who sits on the Judiciary Committee.

No, Senator McCain simply went his own way for his own reasons, and in so doing, confirmed for everyone with a stake in the GOP's future that a McCain candidacy would put a stake in the GOP's heart.

The MSM hasn't figured out yet why the GOP will not fall for the Arizona maverick, and McCain could still create havoc in the election of 2008 if, bitter at again being rejected for reasons he probably cannot fathom, he walks away from the GOP's standard-bearer, a development that his MSM admirers would cheer (as would Hillary and all Dems.)

But even with that risk fully understood, he will not get the nomination.

As for the other four, set aside the conventional wisdom. Before 9/11, Rudy's pro–abortion rights positions or Mitt Romney's Mormon background might have been hurdles too high too clear. But both men have great national security and crisis management credentials.

Senators Frist and Allen are rather conventional candidates, though Allen's governorship and status as a former quarterback for the University of Virginia and son of the late NFL coach of the same name provide the sort of storyline that makes the long march to the nomination easier. Senator Frist has the party establishment's brain trust on his side. Both will probably make it out of New Hampshire to the South, where one will fall away, leaving a three-way scramble.

This is the best thing the GOP can hope for: a knock-down exciting horse race that gets its nominee into the shape necessary to take on the Clinton-Carville-Ickes-Soros machine, and which gives that eventual nominee opportunity after opportunity to debate and take hard questions from Tim Russert and the Beltway gang.

As a participant in or close observer of every campaign since 1976, I can say with certainty that none has been less predictable than the one that looms. Good news for a party in need of a clear succession, and great news for a country in need of a clear impression of an individual who will be a wartime leader.

CHAPTER TWELVE

THE GREAT DIVIDE

This book makes three central claims. First, that the mainstream political left in this country is far more radical than it has ever been in the past. Second, that this newly radicalized political left thoroughly dominates the Democratic Party. Third, because of that domination of the Democratic Party by the increasingly radical political left, it is not safe for the country to entrust any of its major institutions to the control of the Democratic Party.

This is a message that offends many people who are Democrats and who do not believe themselves or their party to be radical. It especially offends some leftists who do not want their agendas accurately described as radical, for fear that it will marginalize their agenda and decrease their likelihood of gaining political power.

But truth should not be a casualty of politics. It may be that the radical left will take the Democratic Party back to power in the House, the Senate, the presidency, or all three. If that happens the country ought to have been given fair warning of the nature of the government they will receive under those circumstances.

The best domestic issue to illustrate this point is same-sex marriage. In September 2005, the overwhelmingly Democratic-heavy California legislature passed a same-sex marriage bill. It did so despite the vote of the people only a few years before banning same-sex marriage, which had passed with landslide approval. Governor Arnold Schwarzenegger rightly vetoed the bill, citing the Proposition 22 supermajority.

While any conservative would have to admit that state legislatures have the right to enact same-sex marriage statutes, and, absent an amendment to the United States Constitution prohibiting such laws, that those laws would be legitimate, the left should also admit (though it wouldn't) that such laws would be "radical" in the truest sense of the word. The California legislature's actions last fall were indeed radical, a departure from the standard of heterosexual marriage that has always been the law of every state in the union since the Constitution was ratified, and indeed the practice of 4,000 years of recorded human history.

Not only did the actions of the California Democrats not shock their national party, whose standard-bearer of a year earlier, John Kerry, had repeatedly and forcefully declared against gay marriage, they went uncommented upon, and the MSM did not even bother to ask national Democratic Party leaders their opinion of the California

Democrats' actions. Not Harry Reid. Not even Californian Nancy Pelosi. Certainly not Hillary Clinton.

In fact, the MSM did not ask, and the Democrats in leadership at the national level did not condemn, because while the Democratic Party mouths opposition to same-sex marriage, it not only does not oppose it, it cheers it.

The scale of the Democrats hypocrisy on this issue is monumental, but it goes unexamined because media elites refuse to focus on such an issue because of the obvious political consequences to the party it prefers.

Media apologists will argue that Hurricane Katrina rendered every other story in America irrelevant at the time, but of course that is absurd, as many other stories continued to "make news" at the time, including the death of Chief Justice Rehnquist, a new federal court decision in California declaring the Pledge of Allegiance unconstitutional, and the confirmation hearings of John Roberts. The decision of the largest single state Democratic Party to embrace as a central issue the cause of same-sex marriage was and remains a huge story, demonstrating not only that state's radical turn, but the radical sympathies of the national leadership and the complicity of the MSM in covering that radical turn in such a fashion as to prevent political damage to the Democrats.

This is just one issue, and it is an obvious marker in the lurch left the Democrats have taken, but it is by no means the only such marker.

Chief Justice John Roberts dazzled the United States when the cameras focused on him during his hearings. Few television commentators recalled that Democrats had for a year blocked even a hearing for Roberts when he was first nominated to the federal bench by the first President Bush, and that a second blockade of Roberts had occurred when the current President Bush made Roberts one of his first eleven judicial nominees in May 2001. That second blockade of Roberts lasted two and a half years!

That is radical stuff, as was the Senate Democrats' embrace of the use of the filibuster over and over again to stop well-qualified mainstream nominees from receiving up-or-down votes. Although this unprecedented obstruction received very little in MSM coverage, new media successfully communicated the reality of the radical tactics in the run-up to the elections of 2002 and 2004, and Democrats paid a price.

The price would have been higher had all of the country truly been educated on what the Dems were up to when Patrick Leahy held the gavel in the Senate Judiciary Committee, or if the real facts of the unprecedented nature of the filibusters been communicated in 2003 and 2004. New media reaches only the politically interested and those with whom they communicate, whereas old media continues to provide much of the information oxygen that a lot of America breathes. Oprah wasn't spending much time on the Democrats' radical left turn. Those who watch only Oprah get a very different view of the debates in Washington than those watching FOX News Channel, MSNBC, and CNN. Oprah's politics are implicit—her travel to New Orleans after Katrina gave us a pretty good understanding of where she sits when the room divides on political lines. The explicit debates on news cable change minds; the implicit politics of entertainment culture leave assumptions undisturbed.

If the assumption is that the Democrats of 2006 are the Democrats of 1966, the Democratic Party is pleased to leave those assumptions alone. The last thing they want America to know is that the party is led by men and women who embrace policies that would have shocked and appalled Kennedy, Truman, and FDR.

Of course the Democratic Party has gone furthest down the left-wing path on issues of national security and the military. The resolve of JFK to bear any burden and pay any price has been replaced by the almost lunatic ramblings of his youngest brother whenever the subject turns to the liberation of Iraq.

The crucial thing to understand is that Ted Kennedy is not the exception within the Democratic Party—he is only its most candid member. If the Democrats return to the White House, it will be to implement the vision of Ted Kennedy, though cloaked in the fuzzy protestations of national security resolve that defined the Clinton administration's fiddling while North Korea cheated its way to uranium enrichment and al Qaeda nested and metastasized in Afghanistan.

On issue after issue, the Democrats have collapsed as a serious participant within the mainstream of American politics.

For more than a decade experts have warned that Social Security and Medicare need massive overhauls in order to survive and serve the senior citizens of this country. When President Bush threw open the door to that process and invited any person to bring any idea to the table, not one Democratic leader brought one idea forward, choosing instead to attempt to gain political leverage. Another two years have thus passed without any progress, and the two major entitlement time bombs continue to tick.

With gasoline at or near $3 a gallon, and with oil passing $70 a barrel, Democrats refused to vote to open the ANWR to exploration or expedite refinery construction. And even with 90,000 square miles of the Gulf Coast devastated by Katrina, the Democratic opposition put union allegiances ahead of rebuilding, and systematically blocked the innovations in contracting and tax law that would have sped relief to the region.

The rhetoric of the Democrats after the storm passed was another key look inside the new party. Representative Cynthia McKinney compared the Superdome to Nazi concentration camps. Not a single national Democrat condemned Louis Farrakhan's assertion that the levees had been blown up. Louisiana senator Mary Landrieu repeatedly exclaimed on the perfidy of the president and FEMA even as Coast Guard deployment teams rescued thousands of New Orleans residents at risk to their own lives, because of the utter failure of the state and local governments, run at every level by Democrats, to conduct an evacuation or provide basic necessities or law enforcement.

Democrats thought that Katrina would prove disastrous for George Bush, but again the new media landscape frustrated their ambitions, and Katrina became the first red/blue storm, with lasting impressions that sorted on partisan lines. As Democrats cheered the apparent ill-effect on George Bush's poll numbers, they did not calculate the impact on the center of the country's opinions on the competencies of Democratic polls.

The overarching question became which party is better prepared to respond—the Democratic Party of Governor Katherine Blanco and Mayor Ray Nagin, or the GOP of George Bush and, yes, Michael Brown?

When the president accepted Brown's resignation but kept the Coast Guard admiral in place, the message was powerful indeed: less-competent people will not be allowed to frustrate our effective personnel. Brown had been up to the task of Category 3 storms that ravaged Florida in 2005. He wasn't up to the task of Category 4 Katrina. He was replaced.

As the churches and synagogues of America instantly organized a massive relief effort for Katrina—an effort of stunning depth and breadth—a Jimmy Carter appointee to the federal bench in California struck down as unconstitutional the recitation of the Pledge of Allegiance in public schools. The same week, Democratic senator Dianne Feinstein questioned John Roberts on whether he could separate his Catholic faith from his judicial work, thus explicitly breaching the

Constitution's Article VI prohibition on religious tests for office—a shocking but candid expression of the core suspicion of sincere religious belief that now animates the national Democratic Party.

New York's Chuck Schumer had launched this tactic against then Alabama attorney general Bill Pryor years earlier, calling into question Pryor's ability to separate his judicial work from his "deeply held beliefs." Pryor's Catholicism was the obvious target of this insinuation. That radical departure ought to have brought condemnation. Instead, it brought allies to Schumer's side to deny that there was anything at all amiss in selectively branding devout Catholics as incapable of judging fairly.

Even when the nomination of Harriet Miers resulted in weeks of intra-GOP and intra-conservative movement sniping, Democrats on the left could not sit back and watch with the glee that professional interest dictated. They too had to attack Miers because of her evangelical faith and her explicit pro-life beliefs, perhaps hastening her exit and the nomination of the conservative Samuel Alito, Jr. Even when silence would benefit their political agenda by prolonging a damaging intra-party feud among Republicans, Democrats could not discipline their own reflexive hostility to traditional faith.

The Democrats' long march to the left began in the opposition to the Vietnam War on the campuses of America and in the streets of Washington, D.C., during the mass protests of the late 1960s and early 1970s. The participants in and allies of the civil rights moment forgave Democratic Party opposition to the Civil Rights Act of 1964 and the Voting Rights Act of 1965, and threw in with the antiwar radicals as opposition to the war spread, and the radicals in the culture wars soon followed on every issue from abortion rights to gay rights to the right to die and decriminalization of marijuana. The radical views on "comparable worth," the radical view first of the threat of nuclear winter and then of the threats posed by global warming were similarly absorbed, as were the radical land-use agendas of the most ardent of the environmentalist activists.

Over and over again, the Democrats adopted the policies of their fringe supporters, but continually tried to wardrobe those turns away from the mainstream in the same clothing that JFK and Truman wore.

Clinton perfected the approach of faux moderation, concealing with skilled rhetoric either radical policy proposals or radical indifference, the former on health care, the latter on national security. The consequence was the triggering of the Republican realignment brought to conclusion by Bush and the untroubled gestation of the Islamist menace, impeded only by a few cruise missiles tossed at abandoned targets. Fecklessness was raised to an art form by Clinton, and the American public now understands the cost of that deceptive "moderation."

As we approach the fortieth anniversary of the fracture of the Democratic Party in the streets of Chicago, 1968, it is impossible to deny that the Democrats in the streets beat the Democrats in the hall like a bongo drum over and over and over again. There is nothing left of the Humphrey forces. Even George McGovern looks moderate now compared to Barbara Boxer and Nancy Pelosi. JFK's breast-beating on the Missile Gap has been exchanged for Ted Kennedy's shouted incendiaries about Bush lies and the malevolence of Halliburton.

The Democratic Party has crossed out of the American political mainstream. It took a long time to do so, but there is no denying that it did. The march was in stages, and the incrementalism went unnoticed or unreported by MSM allies who had also begun their long march at the same time led by their Moses, Walter Cronkite.

Because the media elites were moving in the same direction and at the same pace, they did not notice the direction. But because new media arose, the rest of the country noticed.

The political consequences of the lurch left by the Dems have been disastrous by any measure. They will get worse, provided that the GOP is candid, consistent, and committed to winning big. Unfortunately, this is not a given. In fact, the consolidation of the Bush Realignment depends on the congressional leadership's willingness to govern as a confident and purpose-driven majority, transparent and committed to winning the GWOT, restoring the courts to their appropriate role, reforming runaway entitlements and securing long-term economic growth and the promise of opportunity for all Americans.

The years in the political wilderness for the GOP, beginning in 1932, left the party with a mindset of almost pathetic political cowardice coupled with spasms of ideological Puritanism. The Eisenhower years did nothing to shed the GOP's generally timorous approach to politics. In fact, Ike's overwhelming presence probably arrested the party's political recovery, inducing in the GOP an over-reliance on the top of the ticket and a willingness to live as a minority party in Congress. Richard Nixon's first presidential loss in 1960 taught him a lesson that hardball works and that narrow wins can be manufactured with small margins. He took those lessons into 1968 and began the GOP's era of playing little ball. By the time Nixon was ready to swing for realignment after his landslide in 1972, a disastrous indifference to media imbalance and agenda journalism combined with the deadly embrace of dirty tricks to lead to Nixon's resignation, and with it the crushing of his mandate and the throttling of his realignment.

More wilderness years for the GOP followed until Reagan arrived and taught the GOP how to campaign like a winner, with confidence in the American idea and boldness in policy strokes, and above all, candor about our enemies abroad and the GOP's opponents at home. The "San Francisco Democrats" never knew what hit them. And even when the GOP reverted to little ball in 1988 and 1990, engineering a win here and a win there (a prudence perhaps dictated as much by the perilous transition under way in the east) Bill Clinton proved himself a better manager of little ball politics and little ball government, and stitched together eight years of sound bytes on top of the massive prosperity still flowing from Reagan's revolution.

But that Reagan Revolution had left a legacy in the GOP of policy boldness and aggressive politics—a legacy that Newt Gingrich used, and which George W. Bush embraced and improved upon with an emphasis on good humor and sincere personal faith, neither exploited nor concealed.

This approach works, and not just on election day, but for the country every day. It is proud of America, confident of its place and purpose in the world, certain of its right to leadership and committed to a few core principles. These include the necessity of a strong military that is constantly advancing its capacity, the willingness to confront enemies abroad and strike them if necessary, the advantage to every American of low taxes, and a demand for accountability in government programs with a strong preference for private sector leadership.

The GOP is also very traditional on issues of faith and morals and property. It does not believe that porn or drugs are morally neutral. It believes in God and believes that religious faith ought to be celebrated in the public square, that a city's Christmas crèche is not a constitutional crisis. It believes that people come before endangered insects. It is profoundly opposed to the judiciary's repeated assertion of the authority to dictate to America the results the country must arrive at in currently open and vigorous debates, including those on marriage, abortion, the death penalty, and the rights of public agencies over individual private property.

So profound is this conviction that the Miers nomination set off the first sustained revolt against Bush's leadership, because her commitment to the party's commitments was not obvious to proponents of originalism, despite the assurances of the president and his closest aides. Post-Miers, it is doubtful whether President Bush or any of his successors in the next few decades will nominate any justice who is not already understood by opinion leaders in the GOP as an originalist, assuring brutal battles in the Senate and increasing the need for a filibuster-proof majority for the GOP.

Similarly, the bedrock support for a policy of victory in the GWOT led to a revolt against the Senate GOP. On November 15, 2005, that majority agreed to an amendment to the Defense Appropriations Bill, an amendment offered by Senator John Warner of Virginia, broadly understood to be a rebuke to President Bush, though not one so strong as Democrats had longed for. The Republican base was shocked and disgusted by this hair-splitting and the triumph of politics over purpose. An encore for such weakness will not be tolerated any more than stealth nominees will be tolerated. Though the political leadership of the GOP is lagging behind, the broad base of the party's support has an agenda, and is unforgiving of attempts to shelve that agenda. At its top is victory in the war, but there are many other priorities as well.

Too often the GOP's historic timidity has muffled its voice on all of these issues, a timidity reinforced by the decades-old bias in the MSM that pounds away at every mistake a Republican makes and does not hesitate to frame every issue in the terms most advantageous to the left and hurtful to the right. While this incredible bias remains, it has been exposed and new structures exist through which the GOP can successfully communicate with the electorate, if it resolves to do so.

In fact, the GOP's biggest obstacle is not Nancy Pelosi and Harry Reid's verbal skills, or the policy preference of the Congressional Black Caucus. Far from it. It is McClellan's Disease, and it runs deep.

General George McClellan was one of Lincoln's unsuccessful generals and was eventually Lincoln's Democratic opponent in the 1864 presidential election. While still in command of the Army of the Potomac, McClellan repeatedly blew opportunity after opportunity in the early years of the Civil War to force decisive battles, always overestimating the strength of the Army of Virginia, and always demanding more men and more supplies or imagining obstacles in his way.

Though he was a Democrat, McClellan's timidity has found its home in large parts of the GOP, whose leaders are quick to panic whenever a bad patch of news appears. Even more alarming, there is a refusal to simply debate these crucial issues openly and repeatedly and to demand of media representatives the right to talk not just about what Tim Russert wants to discuss, but what the leadership wants to discuss. The polite courtesies of Washington, D.C., have also seemed over the years to freeze Republicans in stiff silence even as Harry Reid blasts the president as a "loser," or Nancy Pelosi labels him as "dangerous." If politics is understood as football, the GOP doesn't do well in the trenches, and its leaders often lack stomach for contact.

There's a downside for politicians in playing to win. They attract the scorn and ridicule of the opposition. Attacking your own gets the opposite treatment, as Senator McCain's career has proven. If there is one great flaw within the GOP, it is the almost weekly episodes of Republican attacking Republican. Note the party discipline on the other side of the aisle. Intra-party brickbats just don't fly on the left inside the Beltway, though the demand for charging backsliders on the left with treason dominates the lefty blogs.

In the book I wrote during the 2004 election cycle, I asked a rhetorical question: there aren't enough targets that you have to shoot at your friends? It remains the biggest handicap to future GOP gains, as almost any disagreement is grounds for proclamations of betrayal and perfidy.

Sometimes, on rare occasions, there is cause for knock-down battles within the party, but those occasions are few and should be limited to the most crucial of all issues: victory in the GWOT. When Republican senator Lincoln Chafee crosses the aisle to vote with Democrats and demand a timetable for exit from Iraq, as he did on November 15, he ought to have been pummeled by the GOP leadership. When two dozen House members refuse to explore for oil in Alaska because of concerns over caribou, they ought to be named and if they persist in crippling America's national security–driven search for new oil reserves, they ought to be stripped of leadership.

But tax policy and spending policy and a hundred other issues are not national security issues. Differences there ought to be respected and used as opportunities for debate and persuasion, not denunciation.

The meltdown over the Miers nomination was just one such episode of the deep desire among conservatives to attack other Republicans instead of Democrats, and the refusal by some to believe in the necessity of party discipline. Though it was impossible for some conservatives to support Miers in good faith, there was no reason to savage her even before a single news cycle had passed or to engage in the same tactics the Democrats had used to derail the nomination of Robert Bork in 1987. The participation of Judge Bork and George Will in the assault on Miers as well as on the president and his staff for making the nomination was an episode of attempted political suicide. The wounds left by the Miers debacle quickly manifested themselves in shattered party unity on ANWR exploration, tax policy, spending cuts, and even the conduct of the war. Dealing the president a high-profile loss had immediate political consequences, and they were President Bush's fault, and a necessary price to pay to save the Supreme Court from another Souter. Only time and Judge Alito's votes will tell.

The Miers nomination was very helpful, however, in underscoring the GOP's continuing dilemma of political Puritanism. A party, if it is to be a majority, has to be a very big place. Because the Democrats have exited stage left from the political mainstream, the GOP is expanding rapidly and it can expect some vigorous debates. No one "owns" the GOP or its platform. Majorities matter within parties as well as within legislative bodies, and a dead platform is a sign of a dead party. If the GOP throws up a nominee for the presidency or for a Senate seat who is not "orthodox" on all the big issues, the question will not be how to throw him or her overboard, but how to assure that the party rallies to their aid (unless, of course, it is Lincoln Chafee).

Allegiance to party is the only way to achieve long-lasting policy objectives like the defense of country and religious freedom. These are generational conflicts whose resolution will take decades to achieve, and no single politician or one sitting of Congress or Supreme Court will ever "solve" a particular debate because all truly meaningful debates are organic. People serious about politics have to be serious abut parties, and consider not individual candidates or causes, but the parties of which they are a part.

Throughout the Miers debate, I reread the masterful biography of British prime minister Benjamin Disraeli by Lord William Blake, a book widely admired as one of the best biographies ever written about a major political figure. I close where I began, because all the gains of the past six years will be fleeting if the GOP does not commit itself to governing as a majority party, and not as a collection of activists and electeds.

For those who don't know much about Disraeli, it is important to know that he was conservative, a Jew, a novelist, and the architect of the modern Tory Party, which had shattered over a dispute over Britain's restrictive Corn Laws and had failed to regain the people's confidence. Disraeli, via politics, not purity of ideological purpose, rebuilt the machinery and a majority and triumphed over his arch-rival, the leader of the Liberal Party, William Gladstone.

The means by which Disraeli brought his party out of the wilderness was the Reform Act of 1867, a bill that opened the vote in Great Britain to many hundreds of thousands of middle- and lower-class men who had never before voted. It was a radical bill for its day, and even a year before its passage it would have been impossible for most political observers to predict its sponsorship by "Dizzy" and his party. In fact, a few of the arch-conservative Tory members of Parliament left the cabinet over the bill's content, and blasted Disraeli for his abandonment of anything remotely resembling "principle" over the subject area.

In fact, in this debate, Disraeli had no principle more important to him that winning. "A majority is better than the best repartee," he asserted. Blake expanded on this theme:

> The victory Disraeli achieved in 1867 would not give him a thunderous victory until 1874, but even that delayed gratification would not have been possible had Disraeli not ruthlessly put the interests of the party ahead of both personal goals and ideological purity. That long game played for high stakes put Disraeli at the Congress of Berlin exactly at the moment that Europe needed him there.

To be the prime minster in Great Britain is to be the president, the Speaker of the House, and the Senate majority leader. It is much harder to obtain political control in the U.S. than it is in a parliamentary system, and thus much harder to achieve the possibility of legislating an agenda. The party discipline that Disraeli preached and practiced is thus even more necessary in the U.S., and majorities once assembled must be carefully tended to. The desire to bolt the GOP should be resisted at every turn, and the impulse to declare that Issue A or Issue B is a matter of greater importance than party should always be a warning signal that the party that might deliver on A or B, in part or over time, is about to be smashed on the rocks.

There is, of course, an overarching issue in the United States of 2006: the global war on terror. Without continued resolve in this long struggle, a devastating blow will eventually be struck against the U.S. that will forever alter the national government and perhaps even the constitution. We came so close on 9/11 that even speculating on the aftermath of a successful hit on the Capitol has been difficult in the years since that awful day, but no matter how a government would have been reassembled, the use of WMD would preclude a return to ordinary life for an extended period of time.

The Democrats are incapable of this resolve, incapable of seriousness on these issues generally, or on the aggressive tactics that are required and will continue to be required whenever the possibility of terrorists acquiring WMD is real. Because of that reason alone, Republicans have to conduct all of their political calculations against the backdrop of the awful consequences of a return to power of the Democrats.

This is sobering for those who love the game as much as the outcome, or who are particularly attached to an issue they believe is the crucial, defining issue of the day, an issue over which no compromise or delay can be countenanced. There are no such issues, other than national security, even as for Lincoln there were no such issues—not even slavery—other than preserving the Union.

Preserving the Union is the ultimate political objective in 2006, even as it was in Lincoln's day. Today the threat to the Union comes from without, but it is as real as secession, and potentially more deadly than even the Civil War in terms of fatalities. The Democrats simply do not understand this threat. The Republicans do.

That is the Great Divide between the parties. That's why electing Mark Kennedy to the U.S. Senate in Minnesota, and re-electing Jim Talent in Missouri and Rick Santorum in Pennsylvania, are so crucial to the national security.

That's why it's so important to secure the re-election of Tom DeLay even though he is no longer majority leader. That's why getting Ken Blackwell into Ohio's governor's mansion matters so much in 2006 because the Buckeye State in 2008 will again play a pivotal role.

That's why getting the presidential succession problem sorted out quickly becomes so crucial to the GOP's chance of defeating Hillary-Obama, and why self-destructive paroxysms like the Miers meltdown, the House's refusal to pass ANWR exploration on the first try, and the Senate GOP's undercutting of the war effort are the sort of episodes that simply must be avoided.

Even with only a handful of months left in campaign 2006, there are still many opportunities to influence the results in November through contributions and activism. I list and update the key races that can use your financial support at HughHewitt.com, and BeyondTheNews.com remains a center of smart political activism. Please give to the campaigns listed at the former and involve yourself in the latter.

I hope you will find also local congressional races with which to connect to assure that the Republican majority in the House is preserved.

If you have a competitive Senate race in your state, throw yourself as you are able into the fray. Register with the national party at the Republican National Committee via www.rnc.org, and help lay the groundwork for the grueling campaign two years hence.

Make your homepage www.BeyondTheNews.com, where I and others scour the news to present the most important stories and suggestions on citizen response to them. And be prepared to spend a week or two in late October wherever you might be useful. BeyondTheNews.com will be certain to provide information on those needs and opportunities.

Reject the extremes of the party that are always calling on people to leave the party. Get your commentary first, though not exclusively, from the bloggers listed in this book.

If you have children, introduce them to politics. If you find some books to be particularly persuasive, buy multiple copies for your friends and colleagues in the middle. Hold a fund-raiser for a Senate candidate in your home, especially a candidate in a competitive race, even if that candidate is from a state far away from your own.

In other words, work like your party's success depended on you and the country's safety on the party's success.

"GENTLEMEN, I AM A PARTY MAN."

The programme of the Conservative Party is to maintain the Constitution of the country... Gentlemen, I am a party man.

—Benjamin Disraeli

Painting the Map Red is an extended argument on why—in November 2006 and beyond—the American electorate must re-elect and indeed strengthen the Republican majorities in the United States House of Representatives and Senate and throughout the fifty states if America is going to prevail in the war in which it is engaged and from which it cannot retreat without genuine disaster.

If those majorities are significantly narrowed, or if the unthinkable happens and Democrats return to majority status in either or both houses of Congress, America will be deeply weakened in the global war on terror, and the imperial judiciary will receive a fresh license to remake the American culture along the lines envisioned by the narrow leftist elite dominant in Hollywood and the universities.

Winning the GWOT and safeguarding the majoritarian culture in America requires the continuing triumph of the Republican Party, a triumph narrowly won in 2000, but broadened and deepened in 2002 and 2004. In this age of anti-party rhetoric and historical arguments, a defense of party generally and of the Republican Party specifically is not a popular or easy task. It is an era of rote celebration of individualism and an automatic assignment of virtue and intellectual sophistication to "independent" voters and thinkers. Humbug, of course—but that's what is served up daily in the MSM and new media alike, and the "individual" has always been celebrated by the young and by intellectuals of every age.

"Partisan" has become shorthand for "unthinking" even though it is the reflexive dismissal of party loyalty that reflects shallow thought.

"Party discipline" is rarely hailed as a good thing, much less a necessary thing. "Party politics" is MSM code for disreputable politics. Party loyalists are "hacks" who drink "kool aid," their arguments not even worthy of rebuttal (a convenient escape, that trope, for MSM journalists especially who aren't up to the task of arguing specifics). The suspicion about party politics was born a century ago in the Progressive Movement, and party association with Boss Tweed and smoke-filled rooms is an enduring archetype of American history and pop culture.

The disrepute into which party loyalty and party loyalists have fallen is rooted in the MSM's general disdain for everything they generally are not: principled, disciplined, self-denying, and, crucially, significant. To be successful, political parties have to be all those things and more. They also have to be talented and strategic. They have to play to win, and they have to explain—over and over again—how parties operate, and why ideological purity is the great enemy of majorities, and why legislative triumph is often slow in coming, but will never come unless majorities are achieved and maintained.

Reread all of the quotes above. Disraeli was the greatest of the Tory leaders because he rescued that party from irrelevance by first fashioning it into an effective opposition, then by winning a majority in Parliament and becoming prime minister in 1874 (he had served briefly once before). He laid the groundwork for an extended period as the majority party, a period that allowed the British Empire to prepare for the onslaught of the Kaiser and to endure the terrible years 1914 to 1918, and indeed, in surviving that peril, to be there when Churchill emerged from his wilderness to rally the country again to the cause of saving the West.

Disraeli rescued the Conservative Party and retooled it into a modern—for its times—party that allowed the West to survive its greatest challenges of the last century. Disraeli understood the importance of party in a way that most Americans, including most American political leadership, have forgotten.

Now the West is again challenged, and this time there isn't even an obvious center of the enemy's forces. There is no Berlin or Tokyo, no Moscow or Beijing—just a series of websites and sudden, violent attacks of devastating ferocity.

The war will go on for our lifetimes. If Islamofascists obtain and deploy any sort of WMD, the country will never be the same, and might indeed change fundamentally. Though it is less than five years ago, the memory of the devastation of 9/11 has blurred, and many Americans forget just how close a call that was, that the terrible loss of 3,000 could have been tens of thousands higher, and that the government could have been decapitated.

Every single hour of every single day carries the same risk. We are reminded of that possibility by Bali, Madrid, Beslan, London, Amman, scores of attacks in Saudi Arabia and Israel alike, and the ongoing battles in Afghanistan and Iraq. The most important book of 2005, Robert Kaplan's *Imperial Grunts*, is an extended tour of the front lines of the war, made in the company of America's Special Forces and Marines, and stretching from Yemen to Colombia, from Mongolia to the Philippines to Djibouti. The GWOT is as far flung as there are countries and islands and waterways. The American military is up to the challenge. It is by no means certain that the American electorate is.

If Western Civilization does not prevail in the GWOT, does not rally to the cause of free markets and free minds, does not in effect win the argument as well as every battle, a long descent backwards in political time and civilization's advance will follow.

And for the West to prevail, the Republican Party must prevail in American politics for the foreseeable future. Giving power back to the Democrats—in the House, in the Senate, and certainly in the presidency—is to announce first retreat and inevitably surrender in the GWOT. It is like turning the management of a complicated company over to a twelve-year-old. That pre-teen might have the best of intentions, but he will bankrupt the company and destroy its prospects in short order.

The woeful state of the Democratic Party is discussed at length throughout this book, and all but the fever swampers will admit to the terrible trouble the Democrats find themselves in. Its rank and file may still count millions of FDR/JFK/LBJ Democrats among their number. But the Democratic Party leadership went around the McGovern bend long ago, passing the 1972 nominee, in its zeal for anti-American rhetoric and suspicion of American power and purpose. When President Bush described Senator Kerry as on the far left bank of the mainstream of American politics, he was being measured, and he was silent on where the Michael Moore and Howard Dean Democrats make their home on the spectrum of American ideologies.

Most objective observers will admit these facts, but unfortunately, America's media elite—wounded by the rise of new media, but not yet reformed by competitive pressures—persists in pretending the Democratic Party of 2006 is not radical.

Example: in all of American history, no legislative body, state or federal, has ever enacted into law a proposal to allow two individuals of the same sex to marry. The California legislature—dominated by Democrats—passed such a measure in the fall of 2005, but Governor Arnold Schwarzenegger vetoed it. That is a radical departure from past American practice. There is no describing it any other way. But when the MSM did describe the California proposal—very rarely and quickly—it did not assign the term "radical" to it.

That is one of thousands of examples, and many more have been touched on in the chapters you have read. The Democratic Party—as a whole and especially among its national leadership—has gone hard left.

The Republican Party, on the other hand, has remained relatively diverse and centrist, though its aggressive defense of the American idea and its commitment to national security are defining features of the party, as is its commitment to the rule of democratically elected legislatures and executives as opposed to judicially imposed decrees from life-tenured judges and justices.

Crucially, the president and the party he leads has remained trustworthy on the war and on its economic agenda, and reliable as well on the men and women he will put forward for the bench, and which the GOP's majority in the Senate will confirm.

Critics of President Bush and the GOP will at this point explode with rage and Amazon.com reviewers will denounce the book as propaganda. No matter. It is a matter of fact that the proposals generally held by the Republican Party are well within the mainstream of nearly 220 years of American history, most especially those that demand a robust American defense and an aggressive confrontation of global enemies pledged to the destruction of the country.

With the two parties so deeply and significantly differentiated, party politics has taken on a new urgency. The party that governs in Washington—not this individual congressman or that individual senator—matters to an extent we have not seen in our lifetimes. Even at the height of the Vietnam War there remained in the Democratic Party strong and powerful voices that argued for national defense, like Scoop Jackson and Sam Nunn. Even fifteen years ago House Minority Leader Nancy Pelosi would have been seen—by Democrats—as a marginal political figure, something of a colorful nut from San Francisco, and certainly not "leadership" material.

But all of that has changed, and the pace of the march left by the Democrats has increased with each year of the war.

This is why the map has to be painted red, and bright red at that.

There are only two choices for running the country, because Congress ultimately dictates the course of the nation, and Congress is run by one of two parties. All the libertarians and Greens, all the socialists and independents, all the media—new and old—and all the wannabe media . . . they are just the crowds at the sporting event. There are only two teams on the field, and one of them controls the ball.

This is the crucial fact that is lost on most MSM observers and most commentators: there are only two choices on the menu. They are very, very different. There isn't much common ground, nor can there be when the worldviews controlling the two parties are so extraordinarily different.

It is possible for the media to find and celebrate a "centrist" who is the flavor of their month, whether John McCain or Chuck Hagel or— laughable as it truly is—Hillary Clinton. But all the committees and all the subcommittees are run by one party, and all the executive departments are run by one party. A minority party can make demands and occasionally win some concessions, but not many and not for long.

Majorities matter. And they come in one of two colors: red or blue. God help the United States if that color is blue, because the Democrats won't, even though they will think that they are.

So proudly claim a membership in one or the other party and get to the business at hand. There isn't any honor or any significance in standing around the sidelines calling out a play-by-play. There's hardly a journalist or a commentator in the history books who mattered as much as a one-term congressman or even most party activists whose names are forgotten but whose efforts delivered a crucial few hundred votes in Florida in 2000 or Ohio in 2004.

Building the Republican Party—and, by the way, sometimes that means addition by subtraction—is a far more important effort than most every other civilian calling at this point in history. The anti-party elites are either disguised Democrats or simply clueless. Those in the media are the Ted Baxters of the new millennium, and they have no more power to decide the course of the country than Canadians do. Those in the universities have been disappointed not just by recent results at the polls but also by centuries of indifference to their views. The anti-party ideologues of right and left are similarly powerless to impact events, and their volume is in inverse proportion to their influence.

What matters in politics is party, and the party that deserves support in 2006 is the GOP. Garnering that support requires the repeated delivery of some key, undeniably true messages and the adoption of some key and proven tactics.

What does the GOP stand for?

In the middle of last fall's knock-down debates over the war, I fashioned a twelve-word summary for the benefit of my radio audience, and still believe it to be the best guide to the campaign of 2006. While Democrats are chiefly understood as a party of obstruction to whatever President Bush proposes, the GOP remains defined by these dozen words, the four crucial policy steps to achieving a permanent majority:

- Win the war
- Confirm the judges
- Cut the taxes
- Control the spending

If you agree with all, or even most of these propositions, you cannot be a Democrat. And if you take them seriously, you must vote GOP.

It is that simple.

"Gentlemen, I am a party man" is taken from an April 1872 speech made by Disraeli in Manchester, a speech in defense of royalty, and of the Tory Party that defended royalty. Disraeli's great rival, Gladstone, was the prime minister when Disraeli sallied forth with his broadside, and the speech opened the campaign that brought down Gladstone and propelled Disraeli to his years of significance and his leadership at the Congress of Berlin.

Nothing that Disraeli accomplished—and nothing that Gladstone, or Salisbury, or Churchill, or FDR, Truman, JFK, LBJ, Nixon, Reagan, or either Bush accomplished could have been accomplished without a political party raising them up and organizing their majorities and then providing support through their tenures as chief executive of their countries, in war and in peace.

Here is how Disraeli closed his epic address:

And yet, gentlemen, it is not merely our fleets and armies, our powerful artillery, our accumulated capital, and our unlimited credit on which I so much depend, as upon that unbroken spirit of her people, which I believe was never prouder of the imperial country to which they belong. Gentlemen, it is to that spirit that I above all things trust. I look upon the people of Lancashire as a fair representative of the people of England. I think the manner in which they have invited me here, locally a stranger, to receive the expression of their cordial sympathy, and only because they recognize some effort on my part to maintain the greatness of their country, is evidence of the spirit of the land. I must express to you again my deep sense of the generous manner in which you have welcomed me, and in which you have permitted me to express to you my views upon public affairs. Proud of your confidence, and encouraged by your sympathy, I now deliver to you, as my last words, the cause of the Tory party, the English Constitution, and of the British Empire.

Disraeli, wisely, saw his party as a crucial institution in his country's security and prosperity. He was right then, and not just about the Tories, but the Liberals as well.

Parties matter still, as much as any institution in the country, and more than most. It should remain a source of pride to be a party man or a party woman, provided that the party of which you are a member is itself pledged to the high goals of the Constitution the national security, economic growth, and personal liberty.

As the elections of 2006 approach, only one party, the Party of Lincoln, can make that claim.

Vote accordingly.

ACKNOWLEDGMENTS

This is book number six for Lynne Chapman, my assistant now for sixteen years. She has once again shepherded the manuscript from start to finish even as she kept all the other plates spinning!

Sealy and Curtis Yates again provided the guidance and encouragement that experienced and trusted agents do.

The Regnery team has been wonderful to work with. Thanks to Marji Ross, Harry Crocker, and Ben Domenech. My first book, twenty years ago, was with Regnery, and it is great to be back with the most trusted name in conservative publishing.

Many of the ideas in this book have been worked out over the air on the radio show, and the radio show is a product of many hands.

The day-to-day producing and engineering of Duane Patterson—also a fine blogger at radioblogger.com—and Adam Ramsey are extraordinary. Jennie O'Hagan continues to bring new affiliates and new listeners. The assistance of Michael Nolf, Alex Caudana, Austen Swaim, Robbie Haglund, and Anthony Ochoa are also appreciated, as is the volunteer efforts of scores of regular listeners, including Diana, Will, Jamie, Traci, and Elliott. The regular guests on my show since its launch in July 2000 have all helped shape the show and thus this book, even if they disagree with the ideas and the result. Thanks to Michael Barone, Fred Barnes, John Campbell, Erwin Chemerinsky, David Dreier, John Eastman, Frank Gaffney, Morton Kondracke, James Lileks, Katherine Jean Lopez, John McIntyre, Claudia Rosett, Mark Steyn, David Allen White, and, of course, Tarzana Joe and Emmett the Unblinking Eye.

Once again I want to point out the dream team of public-policy professionals who manage Salem Communications' News and Public Affairs Department. Russ Hauth, Russell Shubin, and David Spady help keep Salem's message clear and convincing, and Chuck Defeo and Mary Katharine Ham have joined them in the effort to make BeyondTheNews.com the most effective political news portal on the net. Greg Anderson, Joe Davis, and a legion of station executives have built platforms from which that message can be sent. Ed Atsinger and Stuart Epperson had the vision and skill to bring all these people and hundreds more into the project of building a profitable communications company with a purpose worth pursuing.

Chapman University and its law school remain places of great innovation and talent. Many thanks to Jim Doti and Parham Williams especially, and to many faculty colleagues generally, for creating one of the rare islands in academia where conservatives can flourish.

And thanks, again and again, to Betsy, the perfect partner.

NOTES

Chapter One

1. http://www.washingtonpost.com/wp-dyn/content/article/2005/11/17/AR2005111700982.html.
2. http://washingtontimes.com/national/20051201-121430-4414r.htm.
3. http://66.102.7.104/search?q=cache:TOeqGXXi6A8J:freespace.virgin.net/john.cletheroe/.

Chapter Three

1. http://www.whitehouse.gov/news/releases/2005/05/20050517-2.html.
2. http://www.opinionjournal.com/extra/?id=110006665.
3. http://www.opinionjournal.com/extra/?id=110006633.
4. The Australian blogger the *Journal's* Taranto was referring to is Arthur Chrenkoff, whose meticulous reports on progress in Iraq since the coalition's invasion have been must-reads for

any member of the public weary of the bad news–addicted and devoted MSM.

5. http://www.museum.tv/archives/etv/C/htmlC/cronkitewal/cronkitewal.htm.
6. Videotape, March 16, 2003.
7. Ibid.
8. http://durbin.senate.gov/record.cfm?id=239077.
9. http://english.aljazeera.net/NR/exeres/796AA4AC-531C-4E6F-B855-7FBC52506824.htm.
10. http://english.aljazeera.net/NR/exeres/796AA4AC-531C-4E6F-B855-7FBC52506824.htm.

Chapter Four

1. *New York Times*, June 8, 2005.
2. The Daily Kos, April 16, 2005—post by Armando, "Passive Aggression."
3. Lawandpolitics.blogspot.com, April 12, 2005, post by Publius, "Filibuster?"
4. *Denver Catholic Register*, April 27, 2005.
5. http://billmon.org/archives/001885.html.
6. http://www.mydd.com/story/2005/4/15/1624/35636.

Chapter Five

1. http://eightiesclub.tripod.com/id320.htm].
2. http://dalythoughts.com/?p=2983.

Chapter Six

1. *New York Times*, March 16, 2004.

Chapter Seven

1. http://atrios.blogspot.com/2005_07_10_atrios_archive.html#112151520306119486.
2. http://www.washingtonmonthly.com/archives/individual/2005_07/006733.php.
3. http://www.instapundit.com/archives/016151.php.
4. http://www.weeklystandard.com/Content/Public/Articles/000/000/005/804yqqnr.asp.
5. http://www.opinionjournal.com/columnists/cRosett/?id=110006953.
6. http://strengthandhonor.typepad.com/captaink/2005/07/post.html.
7. http://www.tdctrade.com/econforum/hkma/hkma021001.htm.

8. http://www.truthlaidbear.com/TrafficRanking.php.
9. http://betsyspage.blogspot.com/.
10. http://www.instapundit.com.
11. http://www.powerlineblog.com.
12. http://www.michellemalkin.com.
13. http://galleyslaves.blogspot.com/.
14. http://www.humanevents.com.
15. http://www.nationalreview.com/.
16. http://www.albertmohler.com/blog.php.
17. http://www.johnmarkreynolds.com/weblog.php.
18. http://www.captainsquartersblog.com/mt/.
19. http://www.confirmthem.com/.
20. http://www.redstate.com/.
21. http://www.polipundit.com/.
22. http://www.dalythoughts.com/.
23. http://www.patrickruffini.com/ .
24. http://tks.nationalreview.com/.
25. http://www.mudvillegazette.com/.
26. http://www.blackfive.net/main/.
27. http://www.lt-smash.us/.
28. http://froggyruminations.blogspot.com/.
29. http://www.weeklystandard.com/Content/Public/Articles/000/000/005/
     825ijtne.asp.
30. http://www.boston.com/news/world/middleeast/articles/2005/07/17/
     study_cites_seeds_of_terror_in_iraq/?page=1.
31. http://www.fraterslibertas.com/.
32.   http://www.scrappleface.com/.
33. http://www.lileks.com/.
34. http://www.daybydaycartoon.com/.
35. http://www.tedrall.com/.

Chapter Ten

1. http://www.census.gov/population/www/socdemo/voting/cps2004.html.

INDEX